GREAT EXHIBIT

Graphics

GREAT EXHIBIT

Graphics

BY THE EDITORS OF PBC INTERNATIONAL

Distributor to the book trade in the United
States:

Publishers Group West
4065 Hollis Street
Emeryville, CA 94608

Distributor to the art trade in the United
States:

Letraset USA
40 Eisenhower Drive
Paramus, NJ 07652

Distributor to the art trade in Canada:

Letraset Canada Limited
555 Alden Road
Markham, Ontario L3R 3L5, Canada

Distributed throughout the rest of the
world by:

Hearst Books International
105 Madison Avenue
New York, NY 10016

Library of Congress Cataloging-in-Publication Data

Great exhibit graphics / by the editors of PBC International, Inc.
p. cm.
Includes bibliographical references and index.
ISBN 0-86636-111-1
1. Exhibitions. I. PBC International.
T396.5.G74 1989
659.1'52--dc20 88-3420
CIP

Printing and binding by Toppan Printing
Co. (H.K.) Ltd.

PRINTED IN HONG KONG
10 9 8 7 6 5 4 3 2 1

CONTENTS

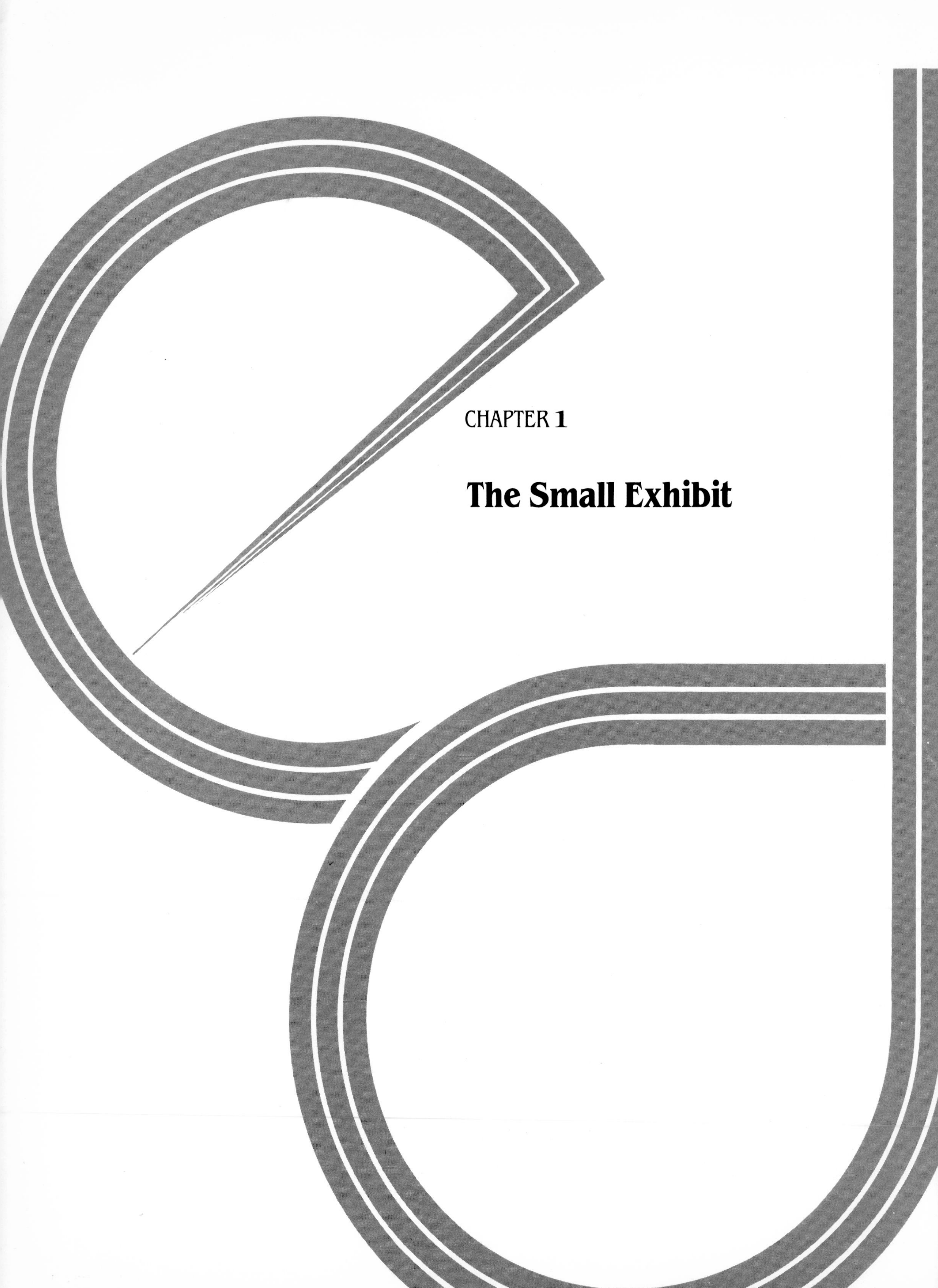

CHAPTER 1

The Small Exhibit

The standard unit at a trade show is generally 100 square feet (9 square meters), although a few shows have standardized on areas that are only 8 feet (2.4 meters) in depth. This chapter is devoted to small booths, which is arbitrarily set at anything that is 400 square feet (37 square meters) or less. This is, incidentally, one of the four size categories set up by the International Exhibitors Association (formerly the National Trade Show Exhibitors Association) for its annual Exhibit Focus competition. We have adopted the International Exhibitors Association's categories for our first four chapters.

The design of a small booth presents special problems. Since show managers generally like to give their central and dominant locations to their major exhibitors, and build out from there, the smaller booths often find themselves on the fringes of the exhibit area.

Many users of small space do little more than hang a sign on the back wall, set up a table or two, and pile merchandise on them. They rely on the existing traffic for visitors to their booth. And since these small exhibitors are often small companies, unfamiliar to those who are attending, interest in the merchandise is the only factor that will lead to a pause at these booths.

These exhibitors tend to forget that the significant cost of participating in a trade show is measured not by dollars spent, but by the return on investment. They also tend to forget that there is a minimum cost of participation. The booth rental, travel to the show, living expenses during the show, and above all the salaries or equivalent of booth staff, are the basic costs, to which must be added whatever is spent to put furniture or a structure in the space. In this light, spending on a display what is, proportionally, a small part of the total cost, is often warranted by the increased traffic and number of sales and/or leads that are created.

While custom exhibits are often used for small-space exhibits, a substantial number of smaller participants have found it less costly and more efficient to turn to the use of ready-made systems or components. These are standard items, produced in quantity, that can be put together in various combinations, to meet the specific need of a particular exhibitor at a particular occasion. Individuality is achieved primarily through the choice of graphics that is applied to the structure, although some of the prefabricated structures can be put together in unusual conformations.

Some systems are adaptations of standard construction, based on the fact that most custom exhibits utilize standard panels as the basic element. These panels, 4 × 8 feet (1.2 × 2.5 meters) being the norm, are custom made. A number of manufacturers design and produce self-standing panels of one sort of plastic material or another. These large, one-piece panels need only the application of graphics, with almost no other shopwork. Molded or vacuum-formed, these panels can be produced rather inexpensively, once the comparatively high initial production costs have been invested. They are, of course, relatively inflexible, and the designer is limited to the sizes, shapes, and colors that have been produced.

At the other extreme is the system that is made up of basic elements, most often linear pieces of various lengths and shapes, with connectors also in a number of variations. These basic elements are put together to produce structures on which graphic panels, background panels, shelves, and other accessories may be mounted. This kind of display is very flexible, and takes the minimum amount of space for shipping and storage. However, unless the designer is careful, the structure tends to overshadow the content. In addition, the large number of individual pieces used sometimes inordinately increases the time, and the cost, of installation.

There are also systems that fall between these extremes. Their basic units are smaller than full 4 × 8 foot panels, and larger and more complex than single rod elements. Their advantages and disadvantages, accordingly, fall somewhere in between as well.

While these prefabricated systems and components have their limitations, often they are the only solutions that meet the restrictions imposed either by time or budget.

exhibitor: Eastman Kodak Company
designer: Giltspur Exhibits/Chicago
producer: Giltspur Exhibits/Chicago

This modular, in-line exhibit was designed for both a 16 foot (4.8 meter) or 20 foot (6 meter) space.

exhibitor: Eastman Kodak Company
designer: William H. Sponn
producer: Kodak Displays & Exhibits Services

With too little room to show actual equipment, the designer turned to using silk screened posterizations. The back wall was refurbished using a modular system produced by Creative Productions 16 years earlier.

exhibitor: Eastman Kodak Company
designer: Exhibitgroup Chicago
producer: Exhibitgroup Chicago

Something old and something new. This exhibit was a reconfiguration of the basic elements of an exhibit used a few months earlier.

exhibitor: Loughman Cabinet Co.
designer: Loughman Cabinet Co.
producer: The Robert Falk Design Group

Since the exhibitor fabricates architectural interiors on a custom basis, there was no standard line of products to be shown. The exhibit illustrated the degree of craftsmanship. One unit, with storage for literature and a slot for information request cards, was a work station, while another had a projector showing selected projects.

exhibitor: Athea, Inc.
designer: Ron Horbinski
producer: Weidig Exhibits, Inc.

The exhibitor, a private label manufacturer, could not show any custom packaging. Using oak tambour and gray ribbed carpet helped avoid the cold, industrial look, and offered a comfortable place to talk with prospects.

exhibitor: St. Louis County Tourism Bureau
designer: J. Lynn Hickman
producer: Walter E. Zemitzsch, Inc.

This exhibit, designed in St. Louis for showing in London, required close cooperation between companies in the two cities. The London group constructed the floor platform, vertical supports, all electrical fixtures and wiring, and handled installation.

exhibitor: Eaton Corporation
designer: Andrew Rokakis
producer: Ohio Displays

This exhibit consisted of 5 × 8 foot (1.5 × 2.4 meters) modules on wheels. Light boxes, panels, headers, and closets all hooked into the modules' slotted backs for easy versatility.

exhibitor: Allied Corporation
designer: Impact Exhibits
producer: Allied Chemical

This exhibit proved how a small space could be divided between related companies by using standard units.

exhibitor: Novatel Communications, Inc.
designer: Jeffrey Raflo/Walker Studio
producer: Ashton Manufacturing Co.

The purpose of the design solution was to draw attention to the company's new mobile radio system. The system was illustrated by an electronic diagram controlled by a computer. Other devices utilized by the exhibitor to gain attention included covering the display with a brass finished metal, using the Exo Plastic Display System overhead, and providing an overhead revolving sign.

exhibitor: Coca-Cola USA
designer: Jeffrey Raflo/Walker Studio
producer: Exhibitgroup Atlanta

This exhibit depicted the Coca-Cola Company's involvement in the black community—special advertising, contracts with black business people, grants to universities, scholarship programs, and career motivational film production. Visuals were interchangeable, allowing customizing the exhibit to a particular audience. Complimentary soft drinks were provided and questions answered by company representatives.

exhibitor: Northrup King
designer: Ed Pehoski
producer: Heritage Communications of St. Paul

This 20 foot (6 meter) unit gave strong company identification. Product information was kept mostly to small, removable panels that could be changed easily.

exhibitor: Dernehl-Taylor
designer: Ron Horbinski
producer: Weidig Exhibits, Inc.

All surfaces of this exhibit were made of pre-finished materials. The inside included two cooking areas an all products were displayed on shelves along the back wall.

exhibitor: Vidal Sassoon
designer: John Wilen II
producer: Dimension Works, Inc.

This was Sassoon's first entry into trade show participation. In addition, the company was introducing a new product.

exhibitor: Wynn's Industrial
designer: Sarah Hansen
producer: Giltspur Exhibits/Los Angeles

Modular units, known as HS-1000, were the basis of this exhibit.

exhibitor: Trade Adjustment Assistance Center, Georgia Tech
designer: Bill Wiggins
producer: Walker Studios

Silk screened balloon fabric was stretched under tension to make the exhibit stand. The lecturn and projection stand were made of Abstracta elements and collapsed flat.

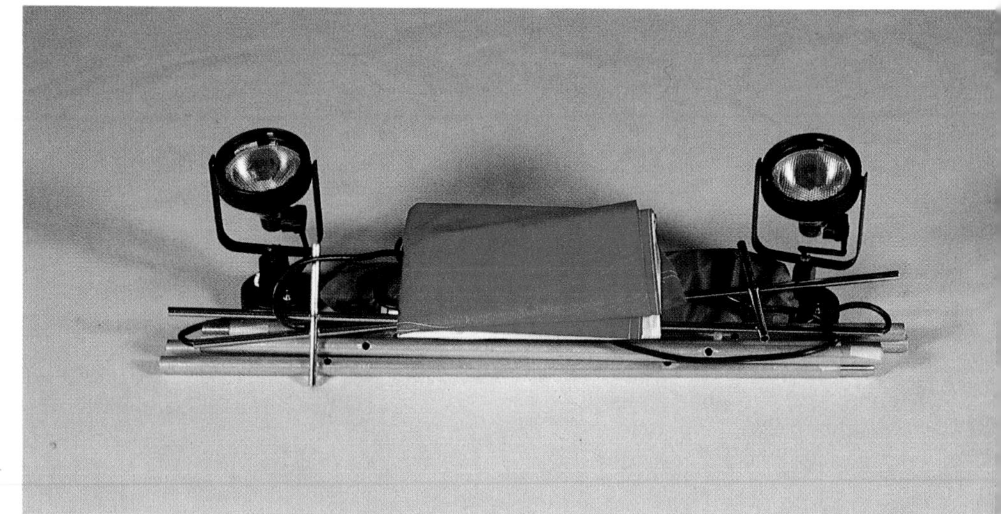

exhibitor: Coleco Industries
designer: Coleco/Outline by Extraversion
producer: Coleco/Outline by Extraversion

The Cabbage Patch Kids is a new line of children's toys. This unit was designed for setting up in department stores.

Richline

Calcitek, Inc.
HYDROXYLAPATITE
... A COMMON AND EXTRAORDINARY SUBSTANCE
EXPANDS PRACTICE CAPABILITIES

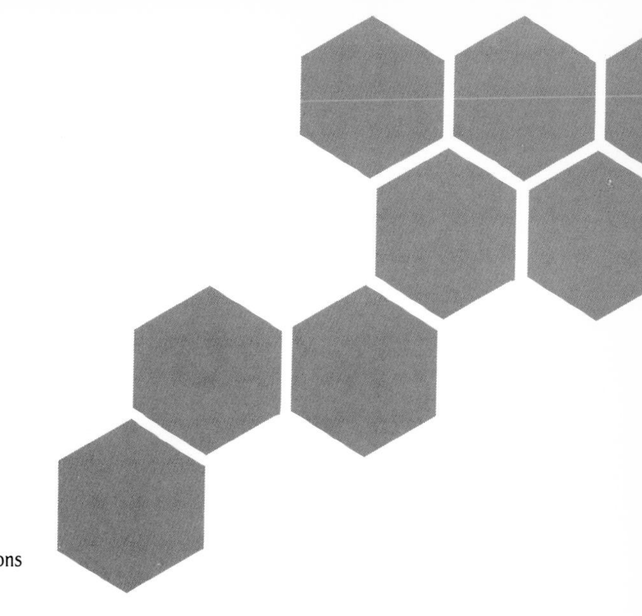

exhibitor: Richline
designer: Fred Calabrese
producer: Exhibit Graphics, Inc.

This 20 foot (6 meter) exhibit could be reduced to fit a 10 foot (3 meter) space if necessary. Storage problems for the jewelry were solved by adding space underneath the units, in the center closet area, and in the end cases.

exhibitor: Calcitek, Inc.
designer: Nicholson Design
producer: Exhibit Concepts

The central portion of this 20 foot (6 meter) linear exhibit consisted of graphic elements sandwiched between sheets of plexiglass. Each element had a separate light, which was controlled by a hand held control box.

exhibitor: Johnson Wax
designer: Norm Polacheck
producer: Hartwig Exhibitions

This exhibit featured a mural of the exhibitor's manufacturing plant, while the products were displayed in an unusual cluster format. The plant shown in the mural was designed by Frank Lloyd Wright.

exhibitor: Eastman Kodak Company
designer: William D. Essig
producer: Kodak Displays & Exhibit Services

Bold, simple graphics, executed on Masonite, were attached with Velcro tape to modular system panels with Velcro inserts, obtained from Giltspur Exhibits/Rochester.

exhibitor: Eastman Kodak Company
designer: William H. Sponn
producer: Kodak Displays & Exhibits Services

The modular panels, with carpet covered inserts, were originally obtained from Giltspur Exhibits/Rochester. In order to register for a prize drawing, visitors were required to watch a demonstration in the booth.

exhibitor: Eastman Kodak Company
designer: Lynch Exhibits
producer: Lynch Exibits

In minimal space, the use of high gloss laminates and polished chrome gave this exhibit a contemporary look.

exhibitor: Eastman Kodak Company
designer: William H. Sponn
producer: Kodak Displays & Exhibits Services

The modular back wall components had originally been obtained from Giltspur Exhibits/Rochester. The headline copy was designed specifically to qualify visitors according to their specific interests.

exhibitor: Pepsi-Cola
designer: Pepsi-Cola
producer: Outline by Extraversion

This unit served as a quickly installed backdrop for presentations that often had to be set up in different locations.

exhibitor: Friendly Ice Cream
designer: J. M. Davis Associates
producer: Cubit Corporation

This 15 foot (4.6 meters) long exhibit used overlay photographs and graphic panels, both which were highlighted by bright eyeball lights.

PONTIAC
712
CAM2
DON Snake PRUDHOMME
DieHard
PEPSI CHALLENGER
PEPSI
GOODYEAR
CHAMPION
TRICK TITANIUM
RAM
CRAGAR
PEPSI

exhibitor: Ward Leonard Electric Co.
designer: Joe Lanza
producer: World Exhibits

This exhibit used vertical blinds for the rear walls, concealing storage space in the center portion.

exhibitor: Keithley Instruments, Inc.
designer: Harry Wok
producer: Gallo Displays, Inc.

The featured products were placed along the aisle, permitting interactive display. Abundant storage space for literature, lead forms, and other information was available in the rear.

exhibitor: ADC Magnetic Controls Company
designer: Harvey Chandler
producer: Heritage Communications of St. Paul

Small products were dramatized by photographs, well identified, and blown up to many times their original size.

exhibitor: Curtis 1000
designer: Jim Walker/Walker Studios
producer: Murphy & Orr

This light weight exhibit was made of eight identical curved 2½ × 8 foot (.75 × 2.5 meter) alucobond panels (one quarter inch thick) covered front and back with hook 'n' loop fabric. They were attached with Voluma connectors. Lettering was made of adhesive backed vinyl. Various exhibit materials were attached with Velcro and double faced tape.

exhibitor: Globe-Union
producer: Hartwig Exhibitions

exhibitor: Novell Data Systems
designer: Pool Displays & Fixture Co.
producer: Pool Displays & Fixture Co.

This exhibit could be assembled into smaller or individual towers for use in smaller shows and demonstrations.

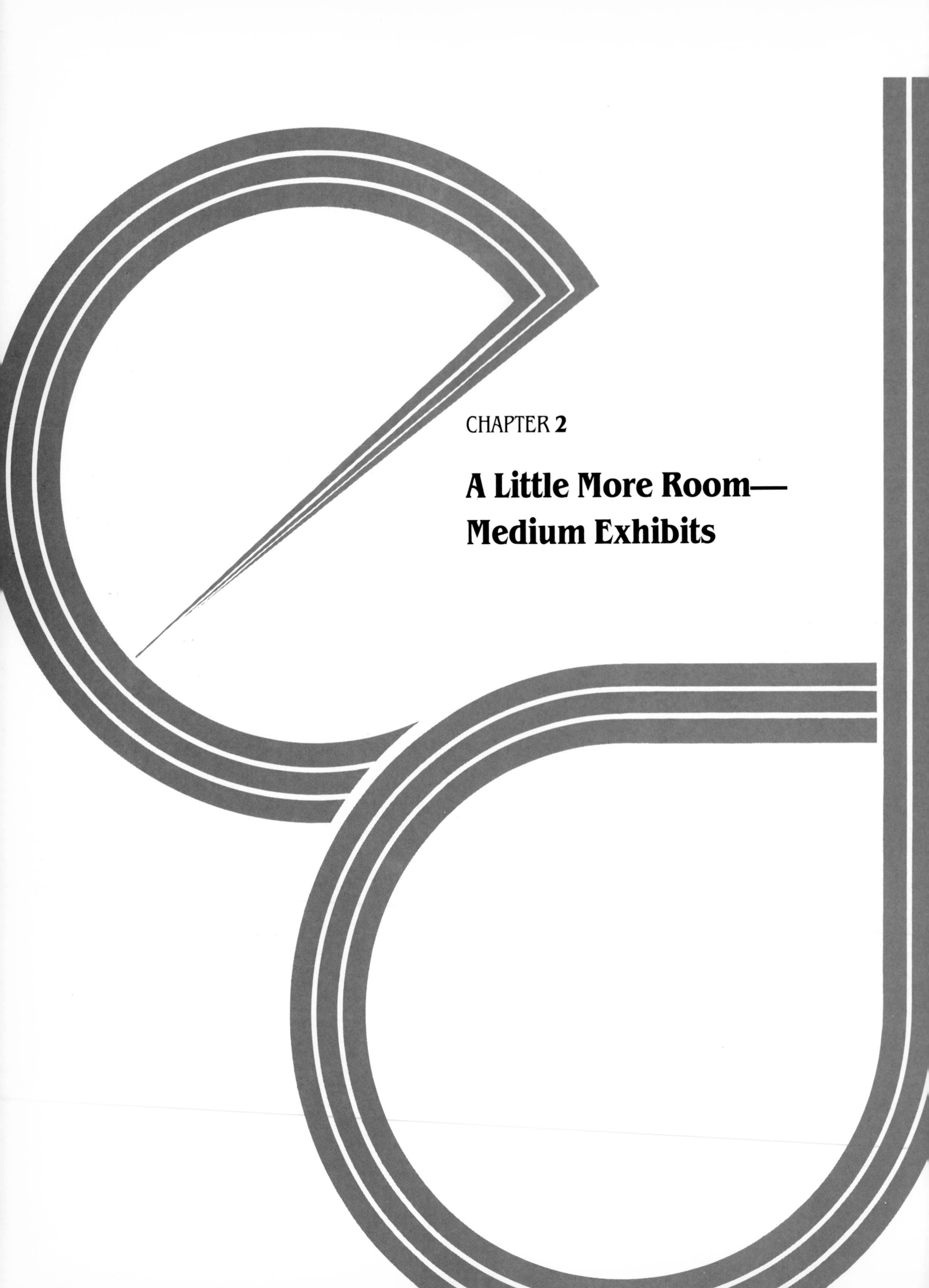

CHAPTER **2**

A Little More Room—Medium Exhibits

This chapter includes exhibits that are bigger than those illustrated in the first chapter, up to 1,600 square feet (148 square meters).

As the space increases, a designer has more scope and, at the same time, more challenge. Obviously, the larger space is required because the exhibitor has more items to show, or there is wider interest in his products. He expects more visitors to his booth and must therefore have more people on duty. This increased traffic means that more attention must be paid to the centers of interest that develop within the booth space. The designer must consider the relationship of one to the other, of how people are to be directed in and around the space.

With these somewhat larger exhibits, we begin to see differentiation in the use of the space provided. While one area might be used to demonstrate a product to a dozen or so visitors, another part of the floor space might be used by a staff member to discuss matters in confidence with a single prospect or customer.

Especially at the upper size limit of this category of exhibit space, we also begin to see the use of two-level structures.

Modular units are frequently used in this category, especially planned so that the area can be broken up into a number of smaller units, for smaller or more specialized shows.

It also is important to distinguish between two aspects of design which are often confused. The first of these is the organization of space, the determination of what will happen in each section of the booth area. Here the designer is concerned with traffic flow, with the kind of interaction between staff and visitor that is to be encouraged, with spaces needed for private conferences, for demonstrations, for storage, etc.

The other phase of design is that involved with surface decoration, including all the graphics, both esthetic and informational. If the first phase is essentially architectural, then the second might be compared to the role of the interior designer. It does not affect basic structure, but is limited to surface treatment. This does not mean that it is of secondary importance, since the primary impact on the visitor, the essential information that is conveyed, is the function of the graphics, the words and illustrations that face the visitor.

Both these functions, the organization of the space and the development of the graphics, should be guided by the exhibitor's objectives, but they need not necessarily be produced by the same individual. The designer who excels at space organization is not necessarily the best at organizing information. In larger shops, the task may be divided.

exhibitor: Hospital Corporation of America
designer: Clifton B. Rockwood
producer: Exhibit 4, Inc.

The Healthcare Express quizzes visitors on their healthcare knowledge using talking computers and other participatory games. A three-year tour is being planned.

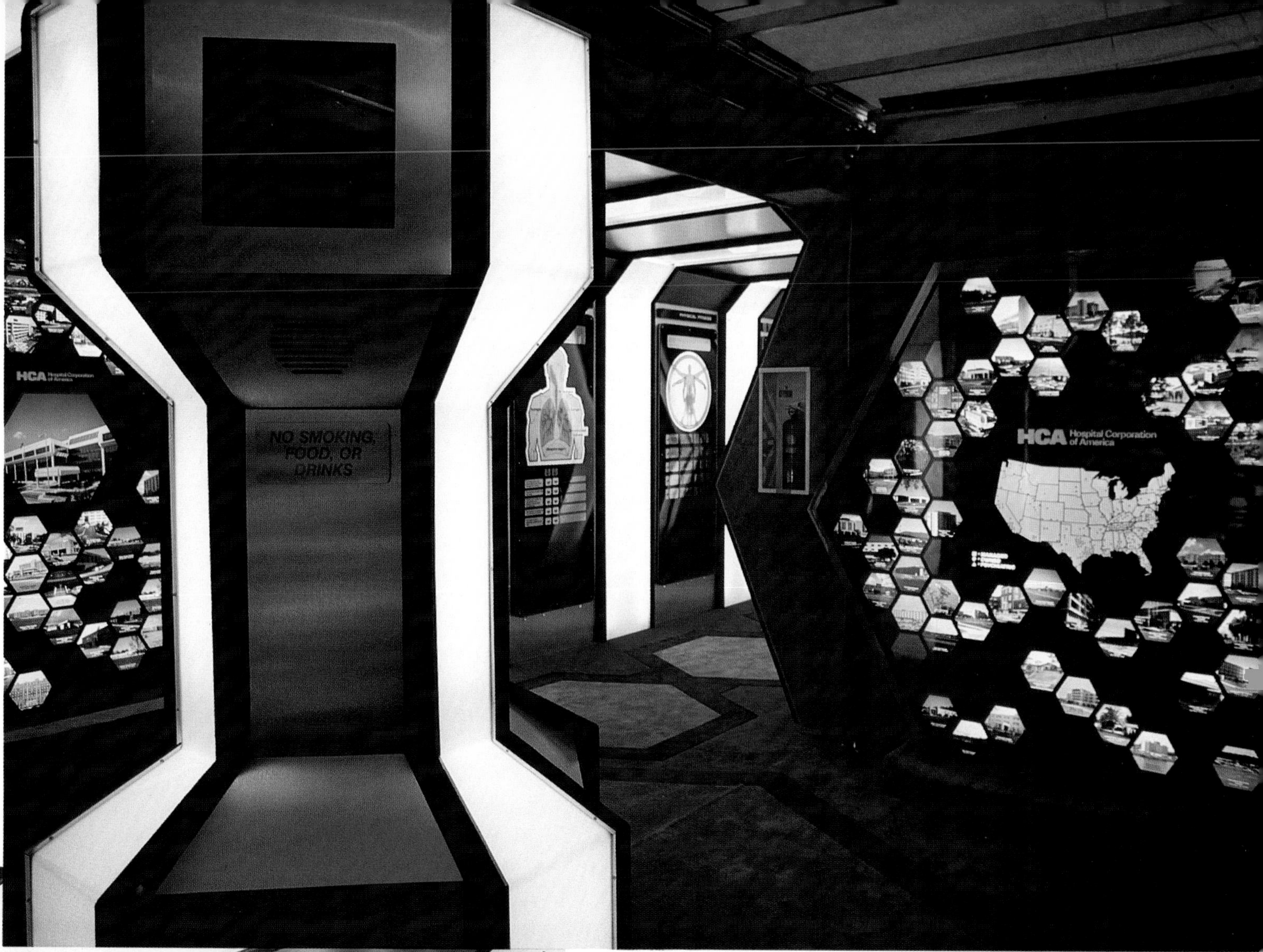
NO SMOKING, FOOD, OR DRINKS
HCA Hospital Corporation of America

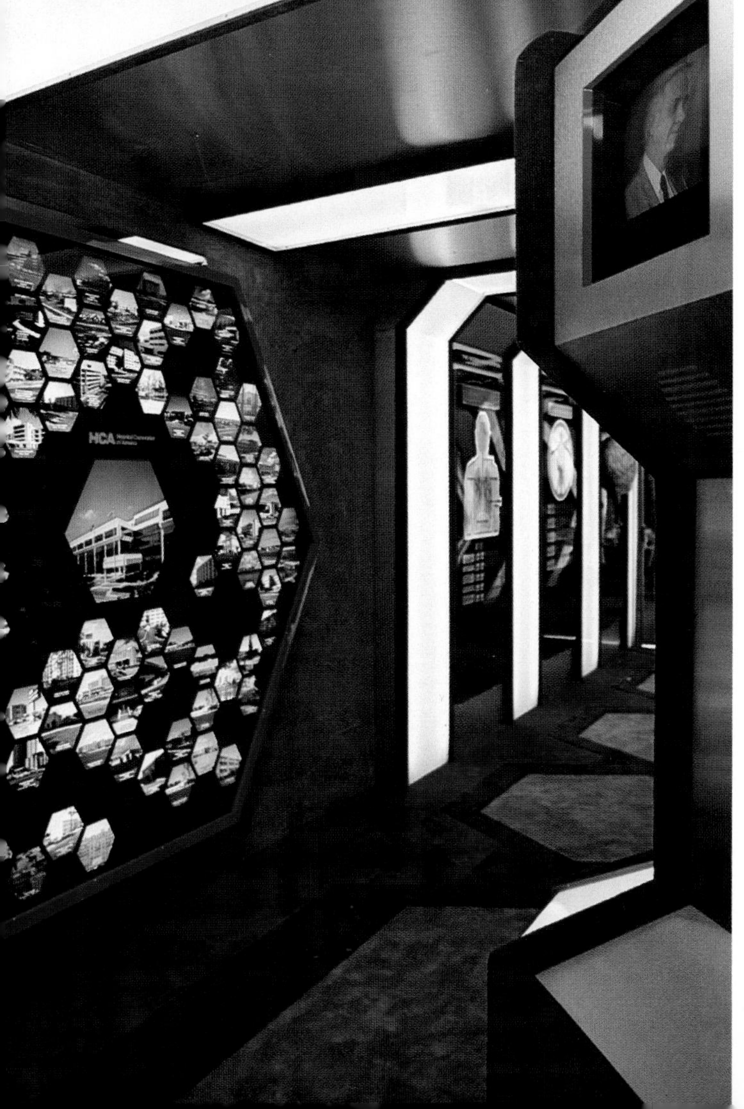

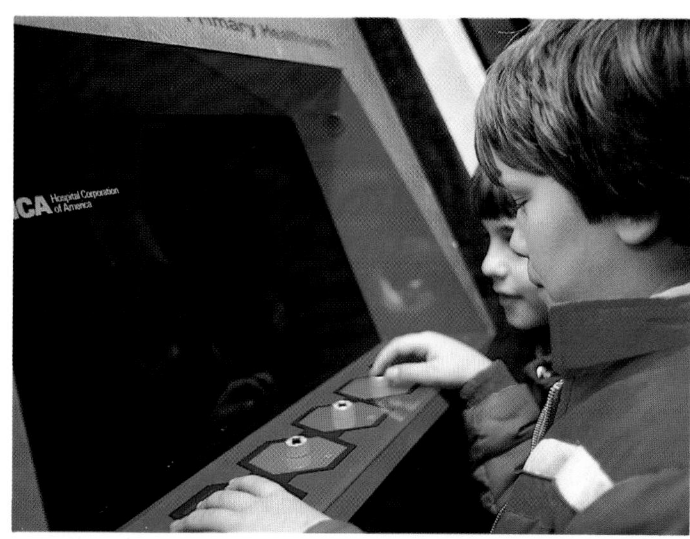

HCA Hospital Corporation of America

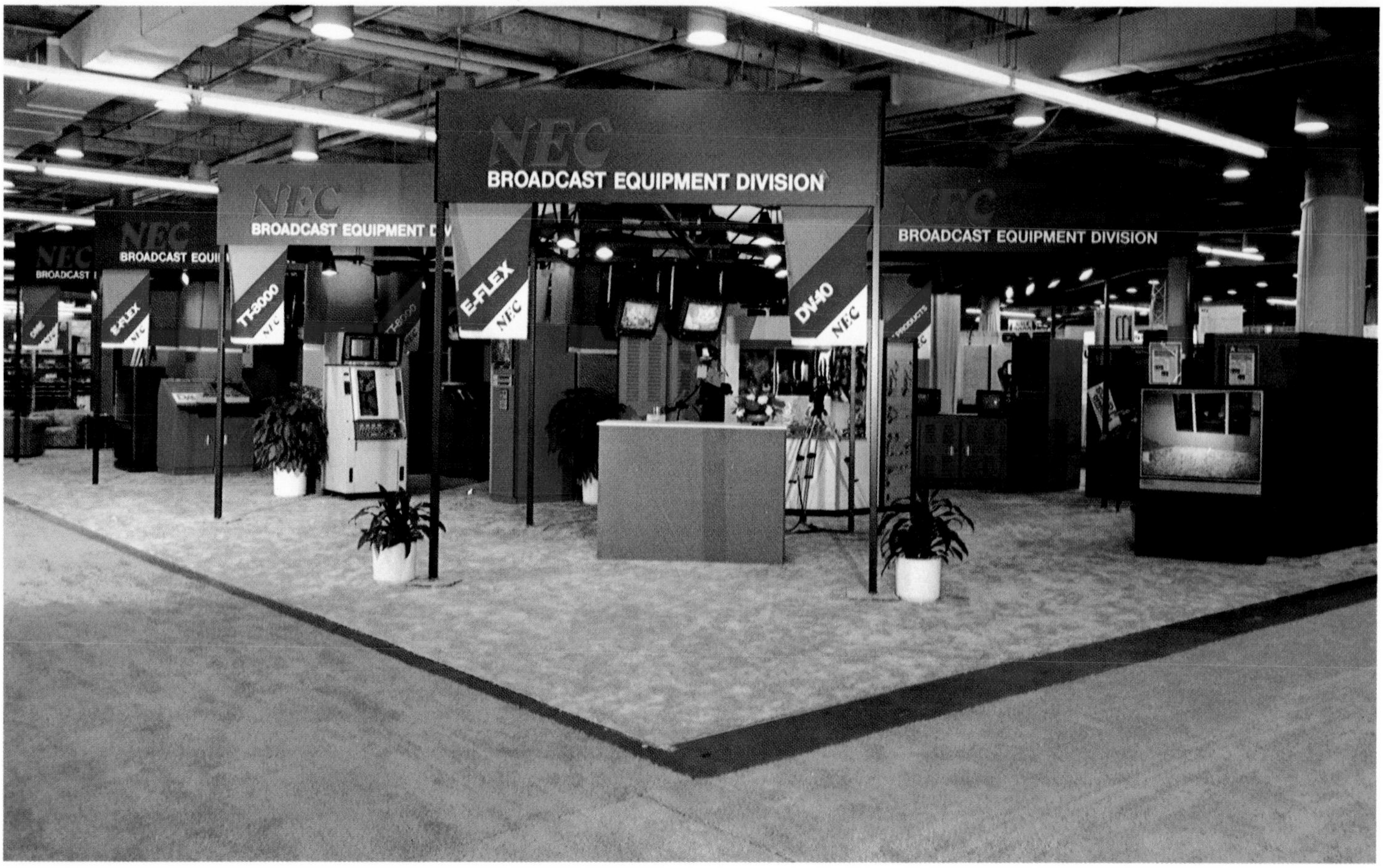
NEC
BROADCAST EQUIPMENT DIVISION
E-FLEX
DV40
T-2000

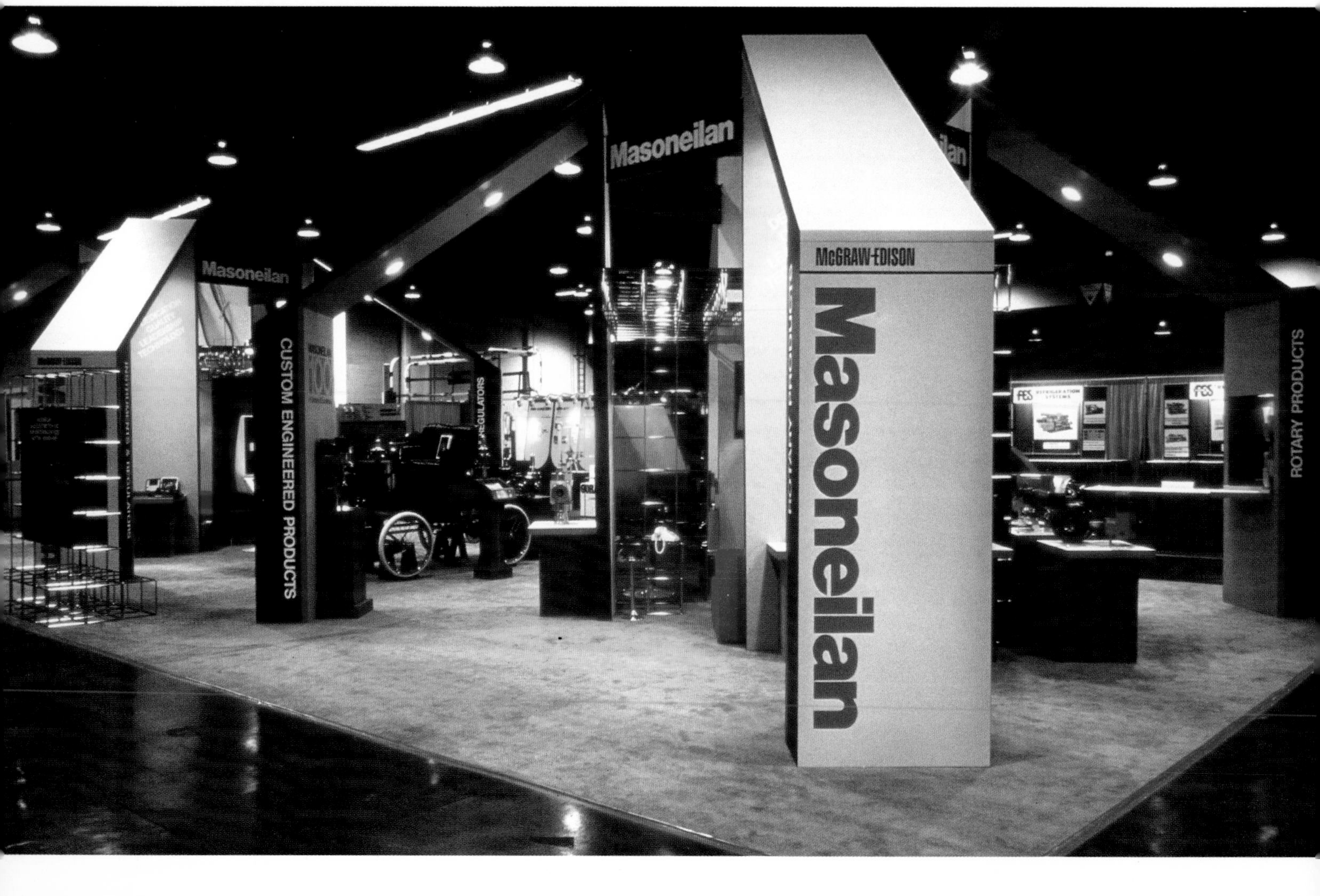
Masoneilan
McGRAW-EDISON
Masoneilan
CUSTOM ENGINEERED PRODUCTS
REGULATORS
ROTARY PRODUCTS

exhibitor: NEC America, Inc.
designer: Bill Hansen
producer: Kitzing, Inc.

This design permitted visitors to find the piece of equipment that interested them quickly and without too many distractions.

exhibitor: Masoneilan
designer: David G. Matys
producer: Berm Studios

Designed for the exhibitor's 200 anniversary, the antiques in the display presented a contrast to the futuristic design of the background.

exhibitor: American Hoechst Plastics
designer: Mike Pierdiluca
producer: Kitzing, Inc.

A demonstration area at one end of the exhibit area was close enough to the aisle to attract the attention of anyone passing by, but viewers had to step within the area to watch. The second level held conference rooms.

exhibitor: Westpoint-Pepperell Mills
designer: Westpoint-Pepperell Mills
producer: Abstracta Structures, Inc.

Using a standard structure permitted this exhibitor to utilize its products as part of the background and display, in a vivid demonstration of fabrics in use.

exhibitor: Norpac Explorations
designer: Design Dynamics
producer: Design Dynamics

The major structural elements were made of solid plywood, sometimes 6 feet (2 meters) thick, covered with Formic. The two curved wings, primarily design elements, were cut from 4 × 10 feet (1.2 × 3 meters) sheets of clear acrylic, held about 1 inch (2.5 centimeters) apart by aluminum spacers and bolts.

exhibitor: Sanitas, a division of L.E. Carpenter
designer: Charles P. Koch
producer: Adex, Inc.

The exhibit used many of the products made by the exhibitor as part of the decoration of the structure. Raised platforms added interest, as did the partially walled-off areas which offered new glimpses into the interior as a visitor walked by.

exhibitor: Storage Technology
designer: Design Dynamics
producer: Design Dynamics

In order to get the massive appearance of this structure, without tremendous weight, the radiating elements were made of canvas stretched over a framework of metal tubing, with interior plywood braces.

exhibitor: Victor Technologies
designer: Convention Exhibits, Inc.
producer: Convention Exhibits, Inc.

The circular central unit enclosed a semisecluded conference area. Large self-standing panels had easily changed graphics and could be arranged to fit varying spaces.

exhibitor: Philips Information System
designer: Tom MacAllister
producer: Giltspur Exhibits/Rochester

While the demonstration counters were lined up along the aisle, individual conference rooms were concealed behind the back wall, reached by an entrance at the corner.

exhibitor: Timplex
designer: Bob Francisco/John Charles McMillan
producer: Admore, Inc.

Open, flexible components could be adapted to various configurations. Audiovisual presentations explained the details of the exhibitor's products.

exhibitor: Litton Industries
designer: Giltspur Exhibits
producer: Giltspur Exhibits

The island areas were used to provide demonstrations, with overhead mirrors to improve observation. The use of the Communicator Modular Exhibit System allowed flexibility in booth layout for future shows.

exhibitor: Timex
designer: Giltspur Exhibits/Boston
producer: Giltspur Exhibits/Boston

Consumer based products were shown in a classic understated design.

exhibitor: Edward Don & Company
designer: Convention Exhibits, Inc.
producer: Convention Exhibits, Inc.

With a long list of items to display, this exhibit avoided a closed-in feeling by using four display cases on the periphery, adding unity and identification with a high central unit supported by four radial beams.

exhibitor: Borg-Warner Corporation
designer: Norm Polacheck
producer: Hartwig Exhibitions

The entire exhibit was made of square units whose bases were made up of four square cabinets.

exhibitor: Hamilton Beach
designer: Norm Polacheck
producer: Hartwig Exhibitions

There were three major demonstration areas on the main level, and since food equipment was being demonstrated, refrigerator and waste disposal space had to be provided. The entire upper deck provided a conference area.

exhibitor: Oilwell, Division of U.S. Steel
designer: Robert Allen Smith
producer: Heritage Communications of Dallas

Technical audiences were impressed by this exhibit, which attracted attention with a full size oil pump and a series of scale models. The brightly colored ceiling was also a definite eye catcher.

exhibitor: Baxter Travenol Laboratories
designer: Michael Grivas
producer: M.G. Design Associates, Inc.

Made up of 10 foot (3 meter) modules, this exhibit featured a secluded conference area beneath a strong brand identification tower. Display cases and demonstration areas were movable and could be placed in various configurations.

exhibitor: Applied Power, Blackhawk & Marquette Divisions
designer: Ron Horbinski
producer: Weidig Exhibits, Inc.

A circus theme helped make even the utilitarian products of this display exciting, with all copy and design done with tongue in cheek. Even the conference room was disguised as a circus wagon at the rear of the tent, while every product grouping had some kind of animated display.

exhibitor: General Exhibits and Displays, Inc.
designer: General Exhibits and Displays, Inc.
producer: General Exhibits and Displays, Inc.

The structure of this island exhibit was itself one of the products being shown at a trade show about trade shows. Also demonstrated were rear and overhead projection, a phone bar, and computer controlled animation.

exhibitor: Westinghouse
designer: Don Graeb
producer: Creative Productions, Inc.

The side walls of this 40 foot (12 meter) van opened out; computerized presentations were given in the interior. The bright exterior graphics were also an eye-catching device.

Bell Helicopter TEXTRON
A SUBSIDIARY OF TEXTRON INC.

Bell Helicopter
TWIN RANGER
FlightSafety

exhibitor: Bell Helicopter Textron, Inc.
producer: Giltspur Exhibits/Dallas

The structure at the rear of this open exhibit had some quiet areas, as well as some secluded briefing rooms.

exhibitor: Alcoa
designer: Dave Klein
producer: Creative Productions, Inc.

Designed for the Paris Air Show, this exhibit featured several separate rooms for personalized presentations and for sales negotiations.

exhibitor: Oneida Silversmiths
designer: Robert Moher/Scott Stewart
producer: Exhibitgroup Chicago

This 32 × 40 foot (10 × 12 meter) peninsular booth was designed to enhance the image of the exhibitor as a leader in its industry. It used plexiglass, both plain and mirrored, to display flatware patterns, which were supplemented by duplicating tabletop arrangements from six respected restaurants.

exhibitor: Stroh's Beer
designer: Visual Marketing, Inc.
producer: Convention Exhibits, Inc.

exhibitor: Abbott Laboratories
designer: Marian Graper
producer: Giltspur Exhibits/Pittsburgh

The basic unit of this modular exhibit is 5 × 8 feet (1.5 × 2.5 meters), primarily used against a back wall. Here the exhibit is shown in a 20 × 30 feet (6 × 9 meter) island space.

exhibitor: Whittaker General Medical
designer: M. Gilbet
producer: The Display House, Inc.

This exhibit used projections on to giant video screens to demonstrate an Apple computer program for hospital inventory control. The elegance and beauty of the setting made a statement by itself.

INTERNATIONAL PAPER COMPANY
INTERNATIONAL PAPE
Confil and Dryfil fabrics for building products
Confil fabrics for apparel and textiles
Stripfil substrates for wallcoverings
Dryfil fabrics for consumer disposables

INTERNATIONAL PAPER COMPANY
From International Paper Company
non woven fabrics

INTERNATIONAL PAPER COMPANY
AISLE 400
INTERNATIONAL PAPER COMPANY
non woven fabrics
What do you need?

exhibitor: International Paper Company
designer: Structural Display, Inc.
producer: Structural Displays, Inc.

Modular units made of molded plastic, with graphic panels applied, added great flexibility and a strong company presence.

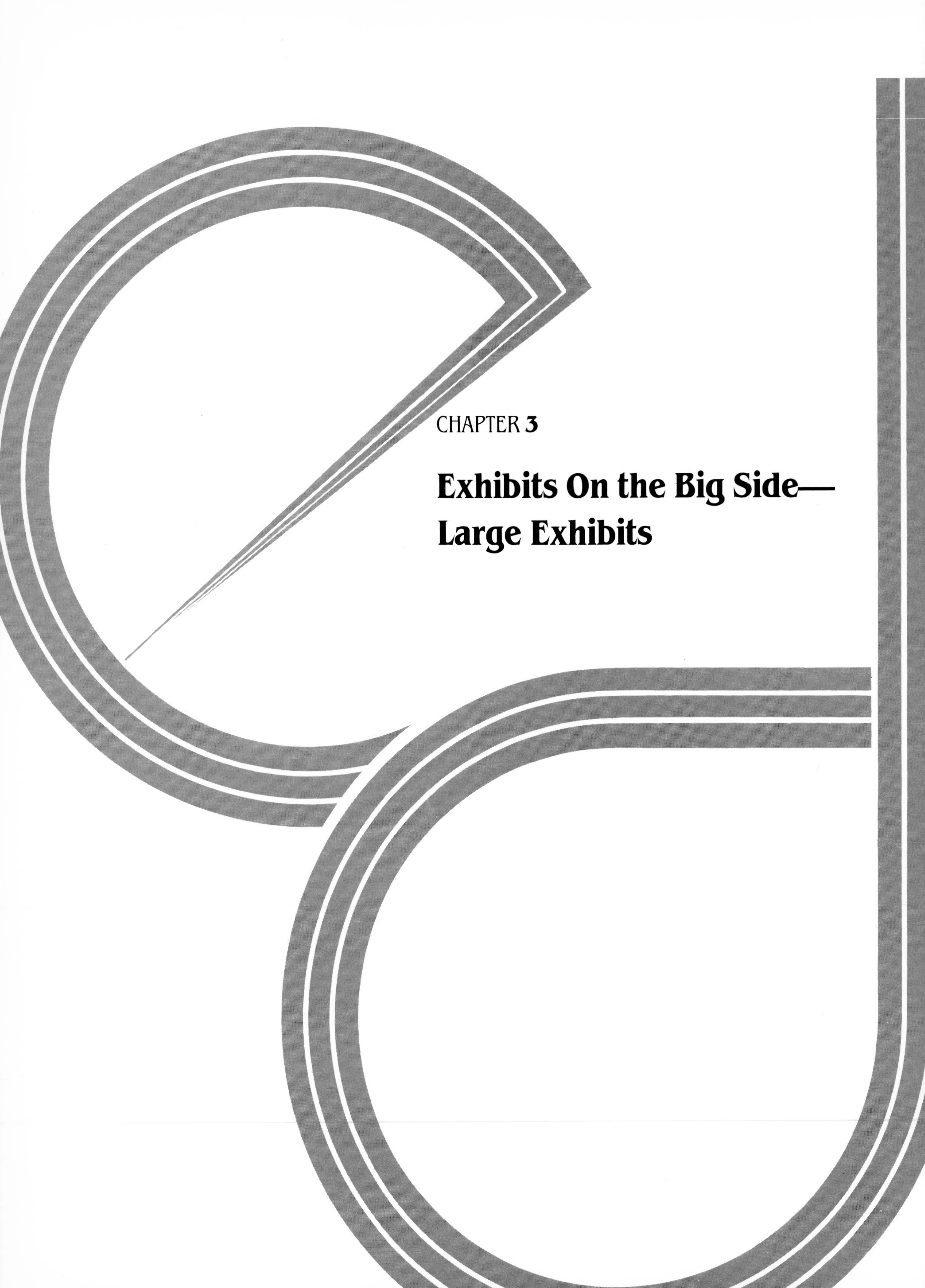

CHAPTER **3**

Exhibits On the Big Side— Large Exhibits

This chapter concerns exhibits covering between 1,601 and 4,000 square feet (149 and 371 square meters) of floor space. Everything we have said about the exhibits in Chapter 2 apply to these larger displays, but even more so.

The larger size of these exhibits makes their design more complicated. There are usually more pieces of equipment on display, each of which must be given an appropriate setting. In addition a space of this size may have two, three, or even four aisle facings, requiring that the designer deal with multiple approaches to the exhibit.

With more people to be handled, an exhibit of this size is likely to incorporate a sit-down demonstration or presentation area. A second floor might also be used for conference rooms, although it is rare that these upper decks will cover a major portion of the space.

In developing the design for such a large area, the designer will most likely prepare a scale model as a preliminary study. It is easier, even for experienced exhibit people, to visualize space relationships, lines of sight, and so on, from a model than from a blueprint, or even a perspective drawing.

As the concept of the exhibit program, rather than the single exhibit, becomes more popular, the project design becomes more complex. The designer must now take into account the need for varying space requirements, varying audiences, varying product selection. The trend is now toward the use of modular units, which can be put together in varied ways to meet these varied needs. This has its effect on the way in which graphics are handled.

Just as the structural arrangement of the exhibit is no longer fixed in the original design, the graphics are less and less an integral part of the construction. Instead, they are increasingly limited to panels which can be removed and replaced. Therefore, updating a product story does not have to involve reworking a major element of an exhibit, but simply preparation of a new piece that carries the new graphics.

However, the exhibitor or his exhibit designer/producer must now develop a method of keeping track of what elements are on hand, what they look like, what condition they are in, and what their scheduling might be. The logistics become important. The exhibits coordinator must be able to pull together everything that is needed for a specific show, pack it compactly, and make sure that no essential element is missing. The greatest problem, it turns out, is that of remembering to include not the major elements, but rather the finishing touches that seem insignificant until they are missed.

Even with modular units, there are certain situations that cannot be accommodated without a rather large variety of individual pieces. For example, you might have three types of standing units, one with both edges unfinished, one finished on the left edge, and the third with its right edge finished. These are not interchangeable, and you simply cannot ship any three to a show. Conversely, you may have both inside corner and outside corner pieces, and you need exactly the right numbers and types for a particular configuration. If the count is not exactly right, you may run into trouble at installation.

Throughout this collection of exhibits, you will find those that rely on modular units and applied graphics, not only in this chapter but also in most of the other chapters.

exhibitor: Hitachi Sales Corporation of America
designer: Mary Scott
producer: Giltspur Exhibits/Sales Promotion Services

This exhibit was set up in four hours using aluminum struts. An upper deck provided individual conference rooms.

exhibitor: Levi's Activewear
designer: Bluepeter/San Francisco
producer: Bluepeter/San Francisco

This exhibit was produced to introduce a Levi first—the company's entry into the skiwear market. The eye catcher was a foam mountain covered in denim and skiwear fabric. The modular units of resawn cedar hold the product line, with show windows on the outside. A stage was provided for fashion shows, and the exhibit was held together by a floor of denim wrapped foam tiles.

exhibitor: Eastman Kodak Company
designer: William H. Sponn/William D. Essig
producer: Kodak Displays & Exhibits Services
Giltspur Exhibits/Rochester

Two helium filled balloons were an inexpensive and eye catching way to create corporate identification. The 30 × 80 foot (9 × 24 meter) space included four presentation areas, each featuring live performers and product demonstrations.

exhibitor: NEC Home Electronics (USA), Inc.
designer: Ben Ami Dresdner
producer: General Exhibits & Displays, Inc.

Video products with 12 to 100 inch (30 to 254 cm) screens were the focus of this exhibit. All of the products were placed in a high tech household environment.

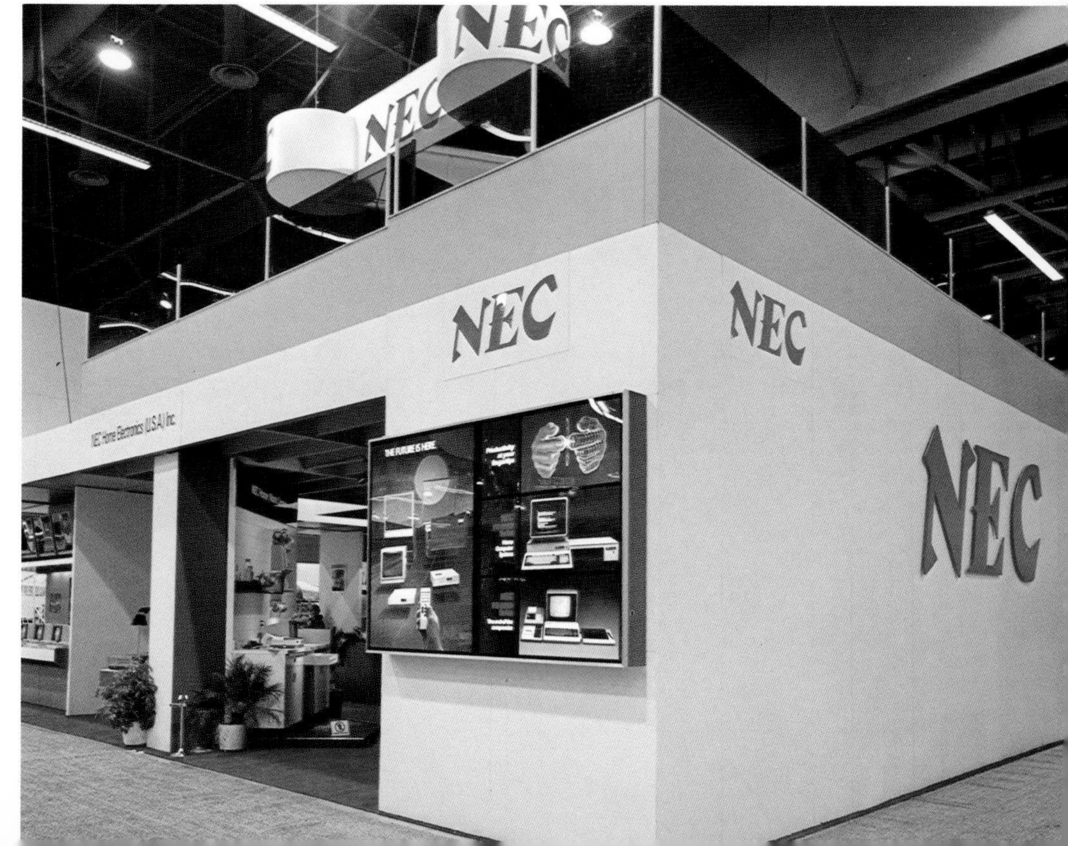

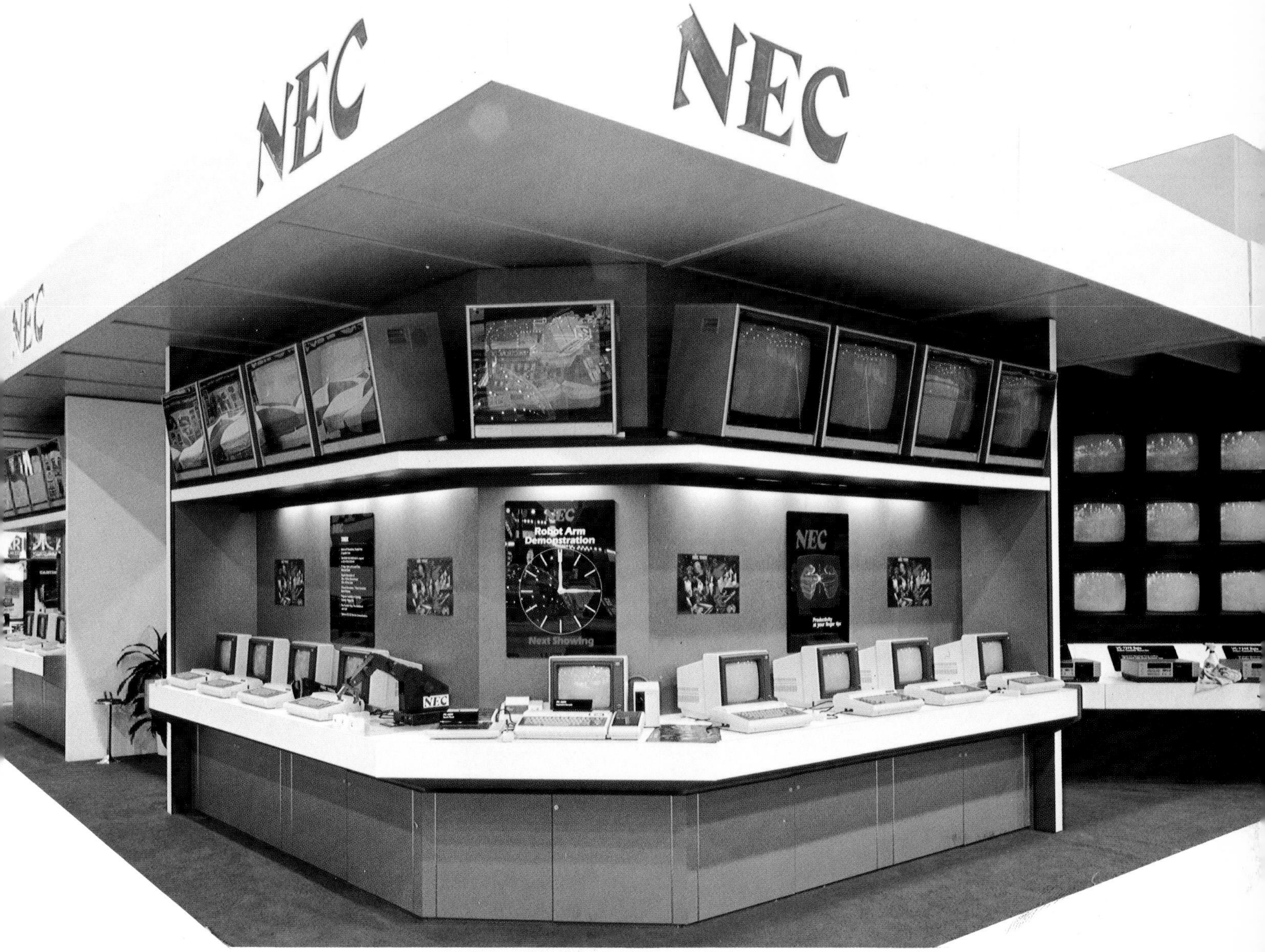
NEC
NEC
NEC
Robot Arm Demonstration
Next Showing

NEC
NEC
NEC
NEC
NEC Home Electronics (U.S.A.) Inc.
THE FUTURE IS HERE

exhibitor: NEC Home Electronics (USA), Inc.
designer: Ben Ami Dresdner
producer: General Exhibits & Displays, Inc.

Emphasizing a little bit of every item, this exhibit placed products in a high tech household environment.

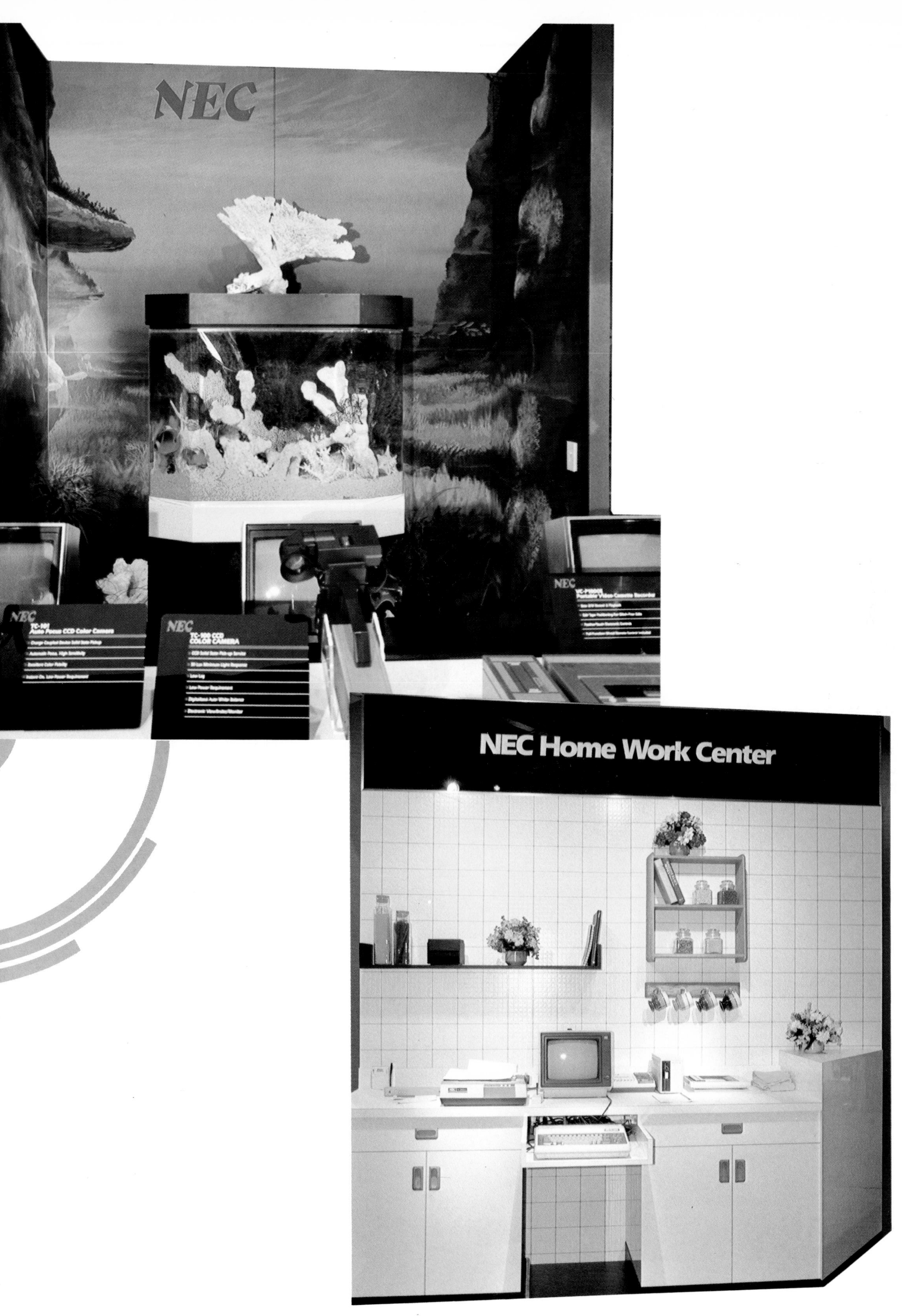
NEC
NEC
TC-101
Auto Focus CCD Color Camera
NEC
TC-100 CCD
COLOR CAMERA
NEC
NEC Home Work Center

AISLE 700
TECHNICAL EXHIBITS
Howmedica
Quality Systems
Howmedica Inc.
Orthopaedics Division
Howmedica Inc.
Orthopaedics Division

Howmedica, Inc.
Orthopaedics Division
Howmedica
TRAUMA
Howmedica
Quality Systems
Howmedica Inc.
Orthopaedics Division
HANDS ON WORKSHOPS
Howmedica Inc. Orthopaedics Division

exhibitor: Nixdorf
designer: General Exhibits and Displays, Inc.
producer: General Exhibits and Displays, Inc.

This structure helped to demonstrate the simplicity and flexibility of modular design.

exhibitor: Howmedica, Inc.
designer: Dennis Moran/Robert Linden
producer: Dimensional Media Group II, Inc.

This two level exhibit, with a conference room on the upper deck, used illuminated 10 foot (3 meter) modular units, in front of which were product demonstration tables. Dramatic company identification was provided by 16 foot (4.8 meter) high towers. The 12 foot (3.6 meter) modules could be rearranged from 20 × 20 foot (6 × 6 meter) islands to one that was 50 × 60 foot (15 × 18 meters).

exhibitor: General Electric Co., Medical Supply Operation
designer: General Exhibits and Displays, Inc.
producer: General Exhibits and Displays, Inc.

While the ceiling offered the light control needed to view x-ray images, the minimum use of ceiling supports permitted greater freedom to place both products and exhibit units on the floor. The carpeted plywood floor enabled cables and electrical lines to be used unnoticed.

GE At the leading edge of imaging technology.
GE先進の画像技術で
GE Führend in der Technologie für bildgebende Systeme.
GE A la pointe de l'imagerie diagnostique.
CT
CT 9800
X-Ray/Digital
Ultrasound
CAPINTEC

exhibitor: Mariner Outboards
designers: Dimensional Displays & Design/ Mercury Marine
producer: Mercury Marine

The unifying characteristic of this exhibit was the rustic surface of the motor stands and other display units.

exhibitor: Mercury Outboards/MerCruiser Stern Drives and Inboard Engines
designer: Mercury Marine
producer: Mercury Marine

exhibitor: Mercury Quicksilver
designers: Dimensional Displays & Design/ Mercury Marine

Arches, mounted on the edges of the exhibit space, helped to tie this unit together. The boundary was also marked with freestanding display cases.

CHAPTER 4

The Giants on the Floor

There are not very many exhibits that fall into this category—greater than 4,000 square feet (371 square meters)—but they draw more than their share of attention. Their very size and rarity makes them memorable, and it is no wonder that they rank high on the list of "most remembered" exhibits.

Usually, because of their complexity, exhibits of this size are built for use at shows that occur at greater time intervals than usual. Obviously they represent a major marketing effort and a major investment. The design process (as well as the design itself) is complicated by the fact that such exhibits usually involve the client at top management levels, and almost always involve the participation of several divisions, all of which must join in the decision making.

This, naturally, stretches out the approval process and adds to the burden of the designer, who often must be the driving force that leads to a mutually acceptable solution. On the other hand, the size of the exhibit and its budget permit greater latitude to the designer, and greater creativity.

The special requirements of the very large exhibit place greater emphasis on one of the problems that constantly face the exhibit designer, the struggle between strength and solidity and lightness and portability. By its basic character, a trade show exhibit is a temporary structure. In this country, at least, an exhibit is built in one location, shipped to a second location, and there it is assembled in a limited time, to be disassembled a few days later, then reshipped and reassembled.

Since on-site labor is expensive, the fewer parts in an exhibit the faster it can be put together and the less costly its installation. On the other hand, when there are fewer parts, each must be larger and this will increase the expenses for crating and shipping, as well as for handling.

An exhibit must be able to stand up under the onslaught of a busy show. It must look substantial, and be strong enough for safety. But can you get the needed rigidity without adding unduly to the weight and the cost? Are there materials and techniques that make positive contributions and still stay within the budget? It is a dilemma to which there is no perfect answer.

Designers are constantly looking for new materials which will help them resolve these conflicting conditions. Producers keep developing systems that have virtues, but always at a price. Sometimes the price is in dollars and cents; often it is in uniformity. The system would be fine, except that its terms limit the number of different ways in which it can be used. The visitor may become more aware of the system than the idea that the display is supposed to support.

Good designers try to keep up with new materials and new techniques. The exhibit industry is rarely a large enough market to support its own research and development. Therefore, exhibit people have to do their own dreaming, to keep an eye open for promising developments, and to see what may be adapted to the special requirements of this industry.

exhibitor: Westinghouse
designer: Don Graeb
producer: Creative Productions, Inc.

This unusual exhibit, shown here in full size and scale model, was designed to permit the exhibitor to present its capabilities in numerous markets to a single prospect, the government of Saudi Arabia.

exhibitor: Bailey Controls
designer: Bob Linden
producer: Dimensional Media Group II, Inc.

The exhibitor's objective was to have bold identification, with a number of demonstration areas. An eight foot (2.5 meter) high metal framework supported a wet-look vinyl covering where two inch deep plastic foam letters were attached with Velcro. The demonstration walls were covered with carpeting to contrast with the illuminated product panels, and to extend the longevity of the exhibit. Within the 130 foot (40 meter) long exhibit were two 10 × 12 foot (3 × 3.6 meter) conference rooms and a large area where a multi slide presentation was shown as part of a demonstration.

exhibitor: Hughes Helicopters, Inc.
designers: Yale H. Pincus/Jack Salley
producer: Exhibit Craft, Inc.

This flexible design could be used with one or two story modules, each of which could hold a helicopter or a meeting area on its second level.

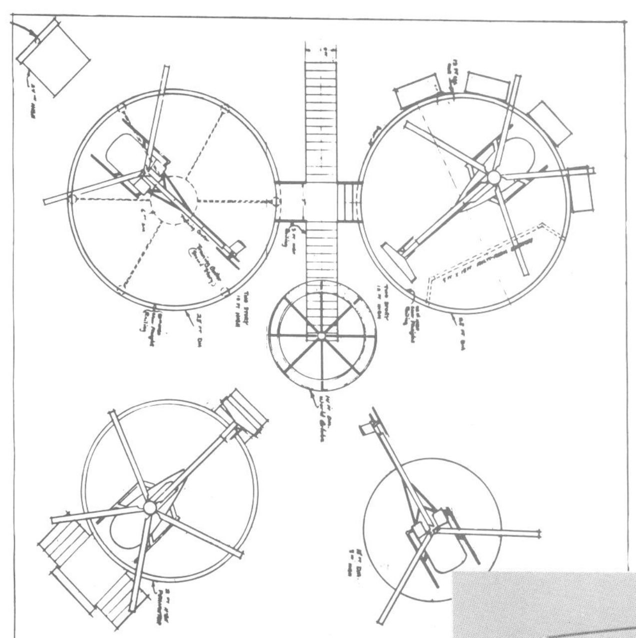

producer: Hughes Helicopters, Inc.
designers: Yale H. Pincus/Jack Salley
producer: Exhibit Crafts, Inc.

In addition to the primary exhibitor, as many as 17 other companies, each with its own products and style, had to be accommodated.

exhibitor: Coleman Company
designer: Davey Packer
producer: Hartwig Exhibitions

This outdoor living exhibit featured a rustic focal structure, 27 foot (8 meter) high, and conference areas on the second floor.

exhibitor: Libbey Glass
designer: Good Displays, Inc.
producer: Good Displays, Inc.

This peninusla exhibit had plenty of room on the main floor to show a complete product line, as well as areas to demonstrate merchandising techniques. The spacious second level held conference rooms.

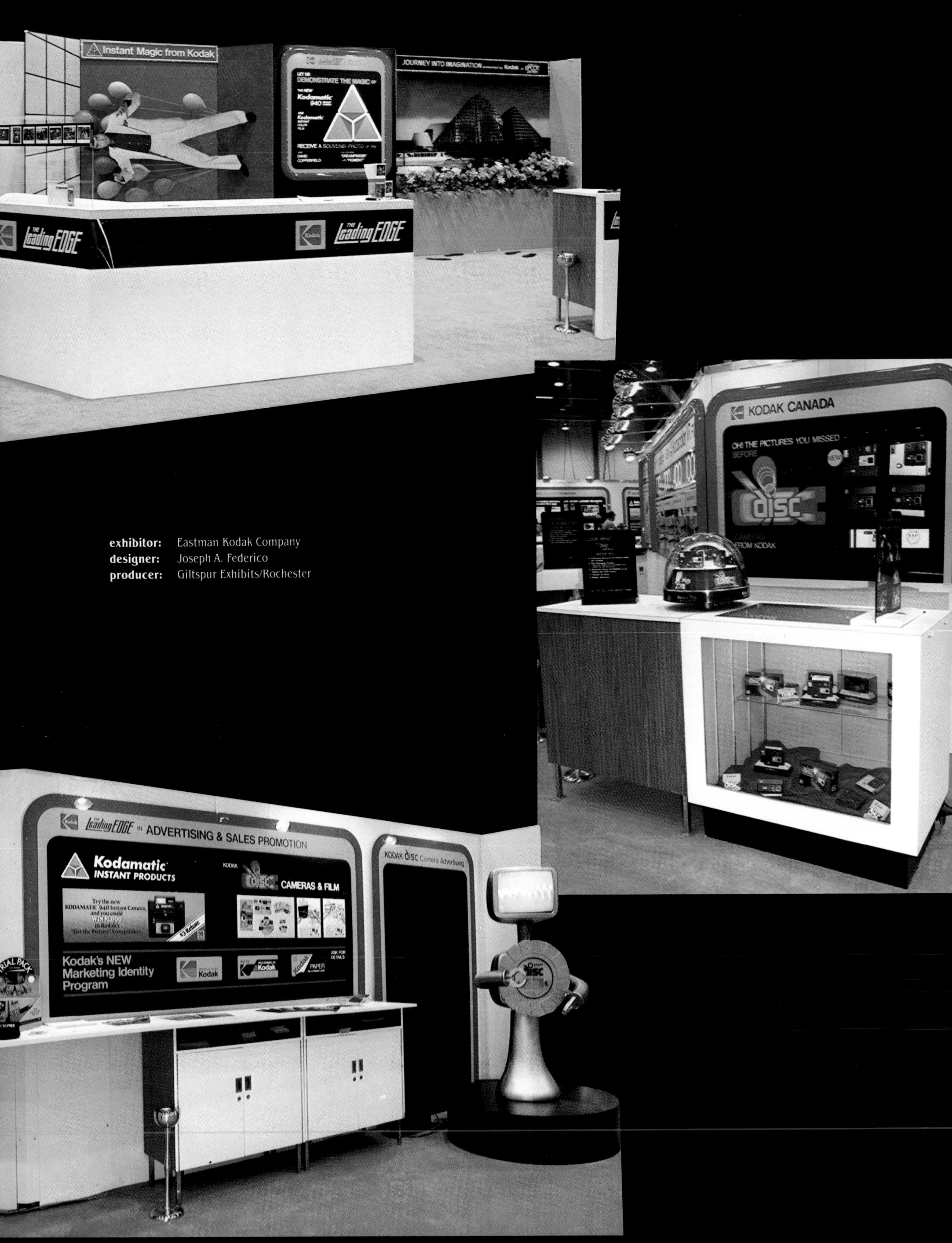

exhibitor: Eastman Kodak Company
designer: Joseph A. Federico
producer: Giltspur Exhibits/Rochester

Kodak The Leading EDGE
We're Going for Gold
in the 1984 Olympic Games
Kodak The Leading EDGE in PHOTOGRAPHIC PAPER & CHEMICALS
We use Kodak PAPER ...for a Good Look
the CHEMISTRY is right
Kodak The Leading EDGE in PROFESSIONAL PRODUCTS
PVAC Kodak Professional Video Analyzing Computer
PRICE
$70,00
F.O.B. ROCHESTER, N.
FEATURES:
DIGITAL IMAGE PROCESSING
SOFTWARE CONTROL
USER FRIENDLY
DISK DATA TRANSFER
NEGATIVE/POSITIVE SYSTEM
LARGE, 3-COLOR HIGH RESOLUTION SCREEN
PROGRAMMABLE ZOO
AUTOMATIC MASKING
ADAPTABLE FILM-HAN
SEMI-AUTOMATIC PROD
FOUR RS-232 PORTS

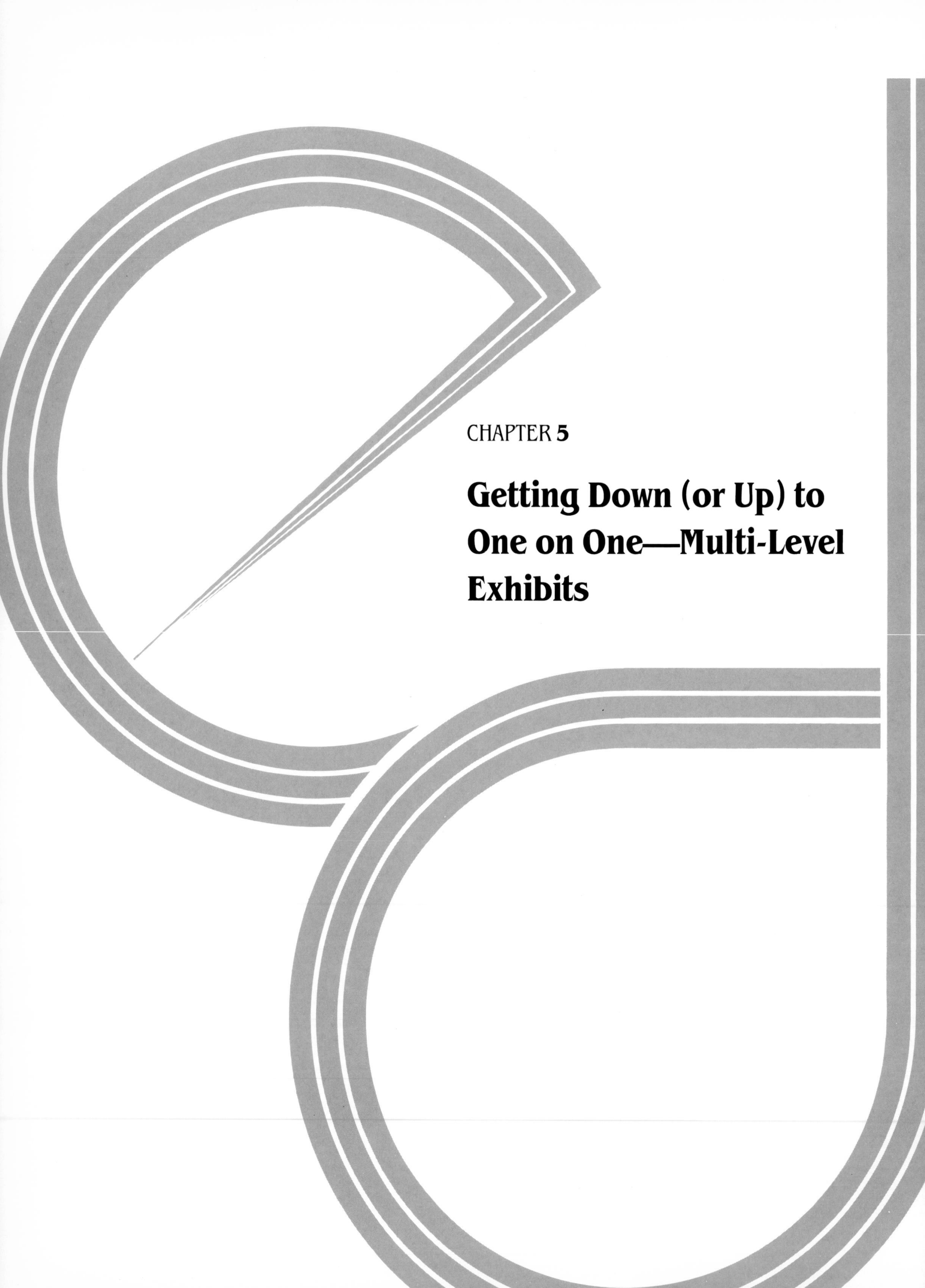

CHAPTER **5**

Getting Down (or Up) to One on One—Multi-Level Exhibits

A trade show is a busy place, its aisles crowded (exhibitors hope) with eager prospects. Most individual booths are designed to be open and inviting. So when there are crowds there are crowded booths as well as crowded aisles.

But not every individual who is part of this crowd is equally valuable to the exhibitor. Some are catalog collectors and information gatherers, and while they may very well be future prospects, and therefore should be treated cordially, they are not ready to sign a purchase order in the foreseeable future. Others are current customers, always a company's most promising prospects.

Discussions with good prospects, current customers or not, can be carried only so far in the public areas of an exhibit. Not only do you wish to prevent interruption, but you also wish to eliminate observation, especially by a wandering competitor.

For that reason, many displays will include an area for a more or less private conversation. Sometimes this is simply a part of the booth that is out of the main traffic flow, with a couple of chairs for a relaxing conversation. In other exhibits, the conference area is completely enclosed and private.

Conference areas are almost universal in European trade shows. This is not surprising, since more business is actually written at these shows than at their American counterparts. That means that all details of a sales contract—prices, delivery schedule, specifications, financial terms—may be hammered out on site, and space for these confidential negotiations must be provided. In addition, European exhibits place a greater emphasis on hospitality functions. Bars are fairly common, and even fully equipped dining rooms are not rare.

As conference rooms become a more frequent necessity, more and more space is needed. And, of course, increasing attendance also demands more space. But space at a show is often limited. When a hall is sold out, show management is reluctant to let one exhibitor increase its floor space if that means squeezing another exhibitor out of the show. The solution: add a second floor.

This adds cost, of course, both in original construction and in installation. While this cost is somewhat balanced by the fact that the basic space rental is no greater for a two-deck structure than for a single-level one, the investment does provide a number of advantages. The most obvious is increased visibility, especially when the number of multi-level structures on the floor is limited. The greater the number of such structures appearing at a single show, the less advantageous they are, since sight lines begin to be shorter and shorter.

Second floors are most often used for conference rooms. It is obviously not easy to entice a casual visitor up a flight of stairs, and usually no such effort is made. Visitors to the second floor are invited guests, and an invitation to the inner sanctum is considered a compliment.

Sometimes upper levels are created "naturally" when the exhibit design requires that some sections on the main floor be shielded from the ambient light of the exhibit hall. This usually happens when audiovisuals are used, especially with the increasing prevalence of video terminals. Since a ceiling must be added over the audiovisual area, it is only a little more costly to use that ceiling as the base of a second floor.

Dual
HITACHI
Dual

exhibitor: Hitachi Sales Corporation of America
designer: Mary Scott
producer: Sales Promotion Services

This modular structure, using a space frame engineered by Synestructics, included a 50 seat theater with a 12 projector presentation. Nine conference rooms were on the second floor.

exhibitor: Blackhawk/Applied Power, Inc.
designer: Ron Horbinski
producer: Weidig Exhibits, Inc.

The central structure of this exhibit was 12 feet wide by 16 feet high (3.6 × 4.8 meters) high, covered in 4 inch (10 cm) squares of high gloss black laminate. The end caps were finished in brushed aluminum. The large neon looking sphere was flat art, rendered in air brush technique with a 3-D perspective. The stairway to the upper conference deck was concealed behind the central structure. "In Shop" set up, using a real car frame, allowed for demonstrations of complete product lines and capabilities. The balance of the booth was occupied by smaller, portable equipment.

exhibitor: Alno
designer: Glahe International
producer: Glahe International

This kind of construction is rarely seen in exhibits in the United States. This European one time set up was for an eight day show.

exhibitor: Sanyo
producer: Giltspur Exhibits

An ingenious use of a long narrow space made this exhibit highly functional. The walls helped to define traffic flow and offered a slight obstacle to curiosity driven visitors. A series of closed viewing rooms on the main level, with conference rooms above, made one on one demonstrations and sales talk easier.

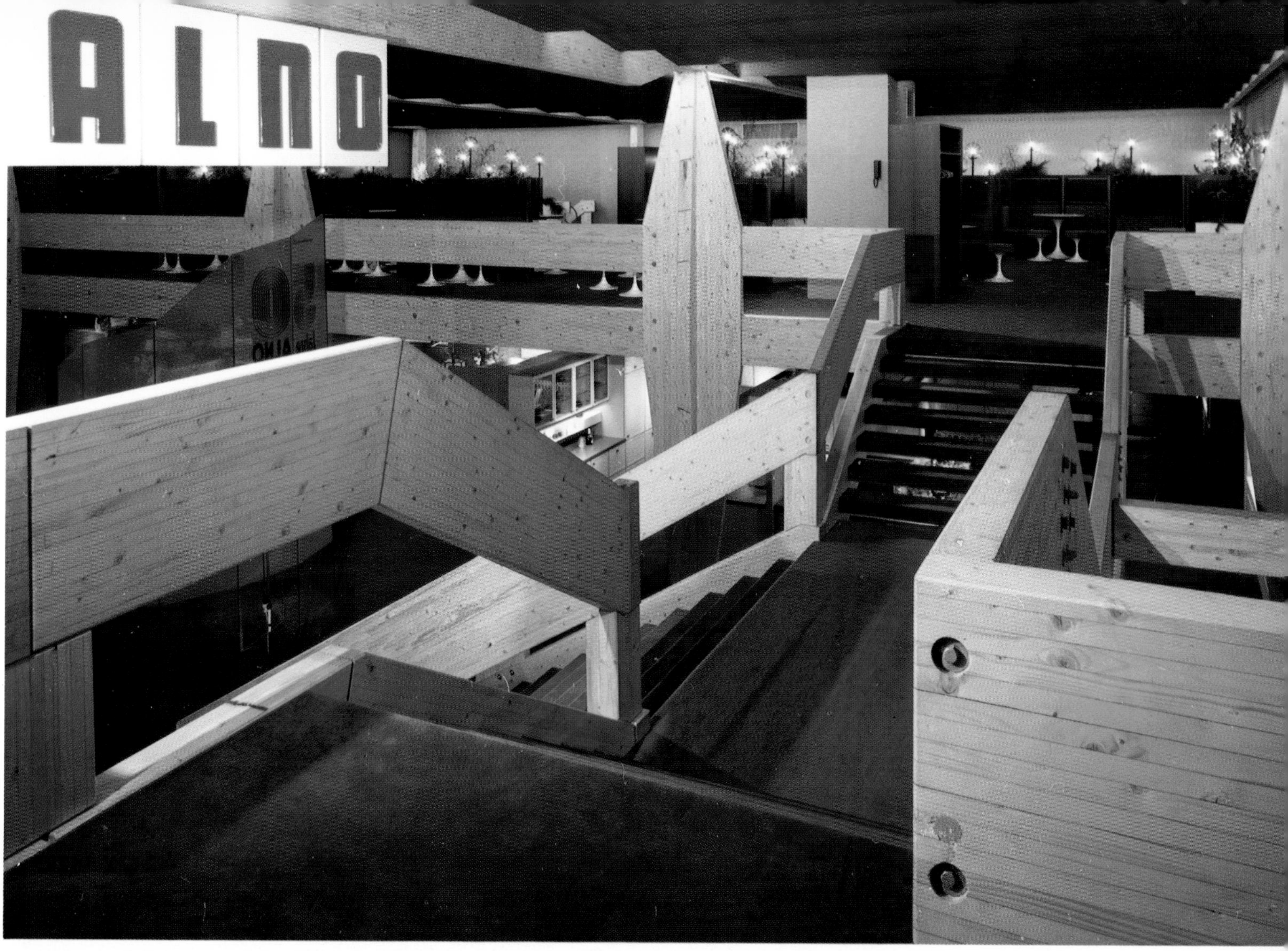
ALNO

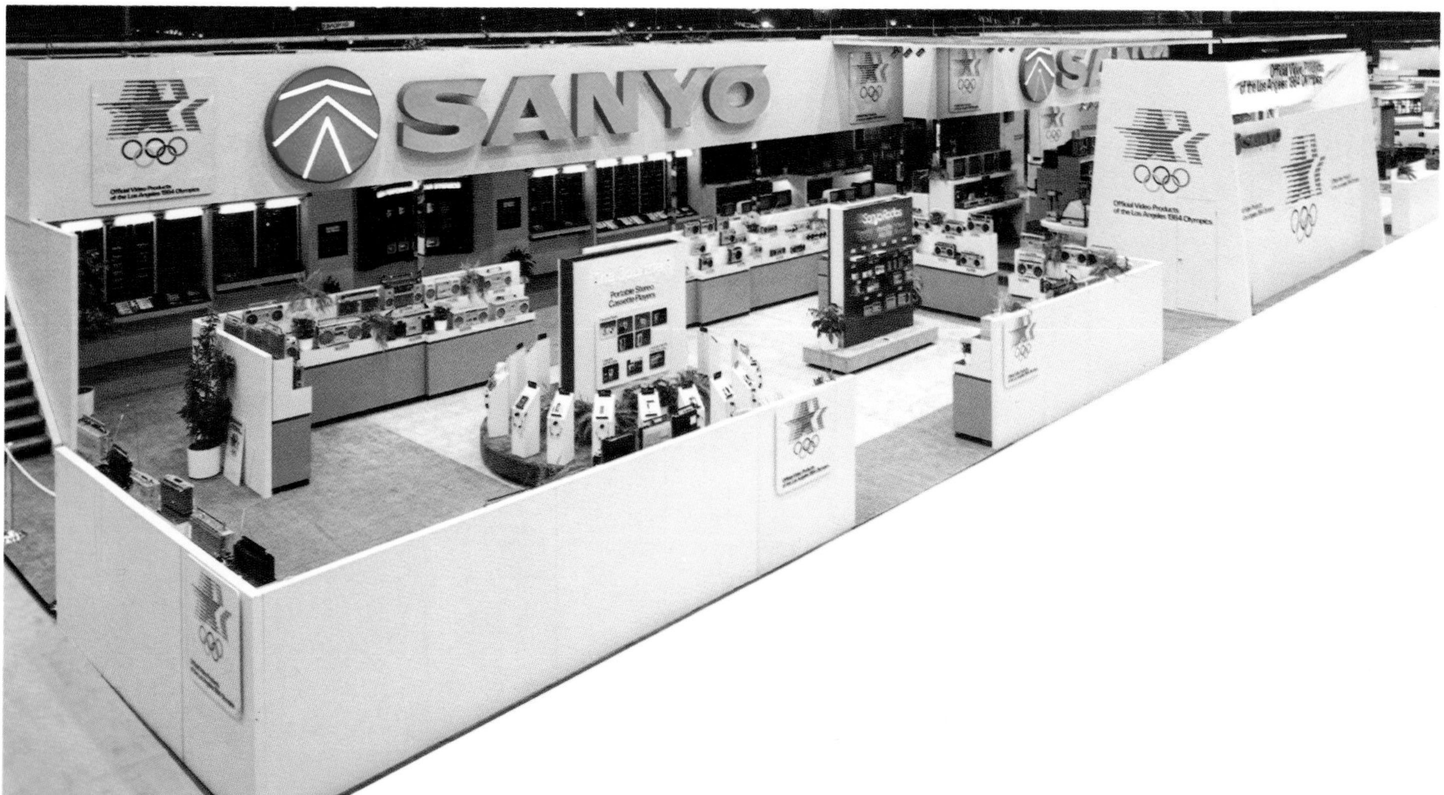
SANYO
Portable Stereo Cassette Players

exhibitor: Eastman Kodak Company
designer: William H. Sponn
producer: Giltspur Exhibits/Chicago

The upper level of the center element, designed for educational seminars, was originally produced by Giltspur Exhibits/Pittsburgh. The lower level of this unit had a large conference room, with four product demonstration areas. Perimeter units featured selling and information stations.

Kodak
It's in the Stars
Shining Star of COM

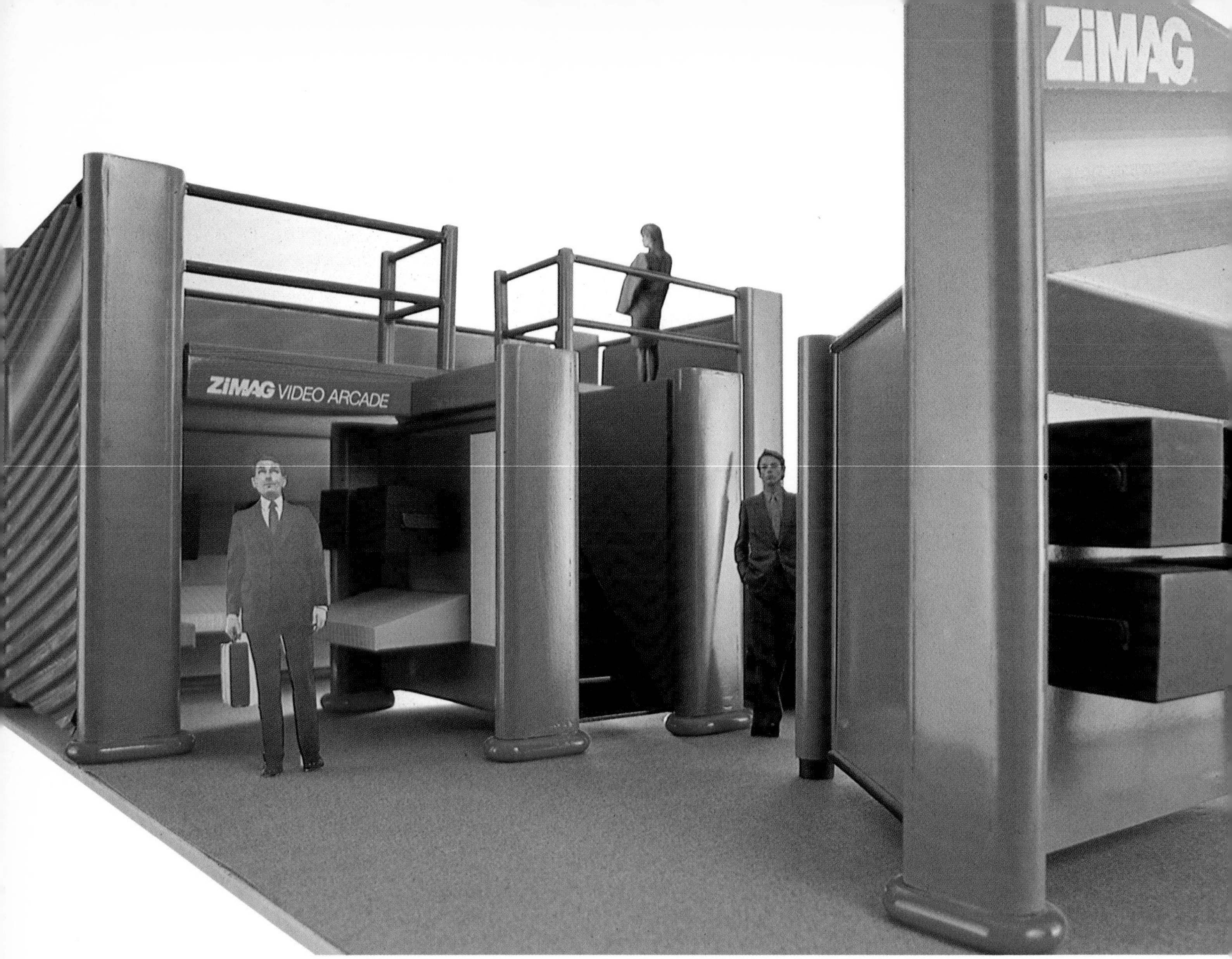

ZIMAG VIDEO

exhibitor: Magnetic Tape Internaional (ZIMAG)
designers: Mary Scott/Frank Maddocks
producers: Giltspur Exhibits/Sales Promotion Services

The unique design, which included a video arcade and conference area, established the exhibitor as a new force in its marketplace.

exhibitor:	CGR Medical Corporation
designer:	Ron Ferguson
producer:	Exhibit Group Chicago

This multi-level structure set up at the Radiological Society of North America show was used to exhibit radiological diagnosis imaging equipment. Ten complete x-ray systems were designed, as were a new ultrason unit and radiotherapy rotating couch. Three conference areas, two open and one closed, were located on the upper levels.

exhibitor: AGFA-Gavaert Rex, Inc.
designer: Structural Display, Inc.
producer: Structural Display, Inc.

The external structure of this two story exhibit not only served as an eye-catching device on the show floor, but gave a modern high tech feeling.

exhibitor: Kohler
designer: Alfred Gluckman (Design Form Exhibit Corp.)
producer: Convention Exhibits/Material Expressions

This exhibit, with its bright lights and multi-levels, was a real eye catcher.

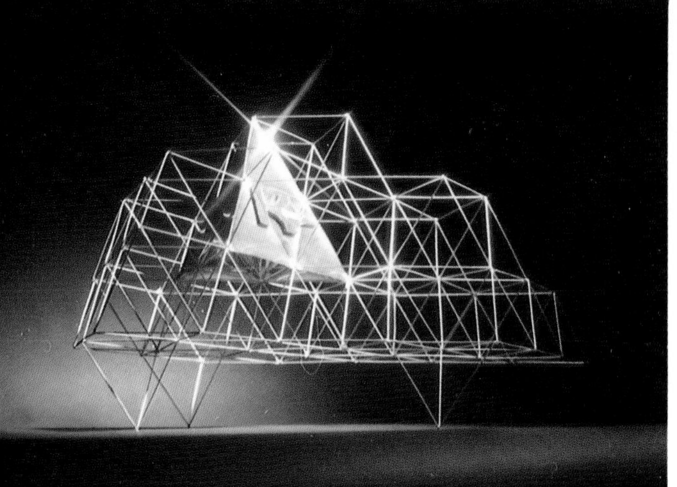

exhibitor: Kearney
designer: Bob Naas/Walker Studio
producer: Malone Displays

The tetrahedral space frame was used to symbolize the theme "Building Products for Power Distribution," as well as to achieve a commanding presence on the exhibit floor.

exhibitor: Solvay
designer: Glahe International
producer: Glahe International

This exhibitor used the second level as a full service restaurant and lounge for its major prospects, a common custom at large European fairs.

exhibitor: Xerox
designer: Ray Crouch
producer: Giltspur Exhibits/Rochester

The key to this exhibit that showed a network system was a stage area with three levels. A 14 foot (4 meter) technical grid whose sequential lighting of transparencies supported neighboring demos was also utilized.

XEROX
Office Systems

exhibitor: Gemco-Ware, Inc.
producer: Stevens Exhibits

The exhibitor's "country store" look had won prizes, but more space was needed and could only be obtained by going to a multi-level structure. The new design retained the warmth and charm of the previous one while adding the necessary space.

exhibitor: Ekco Housewares
designer: Fred Kitzing
producer: Kitzing, Inc.

The wood chosen for the dividers and the bases in this exhibit form a fine contrast for the items on display, mostly of gleaming metal. The second deck conference area is convenient, yet secluded.

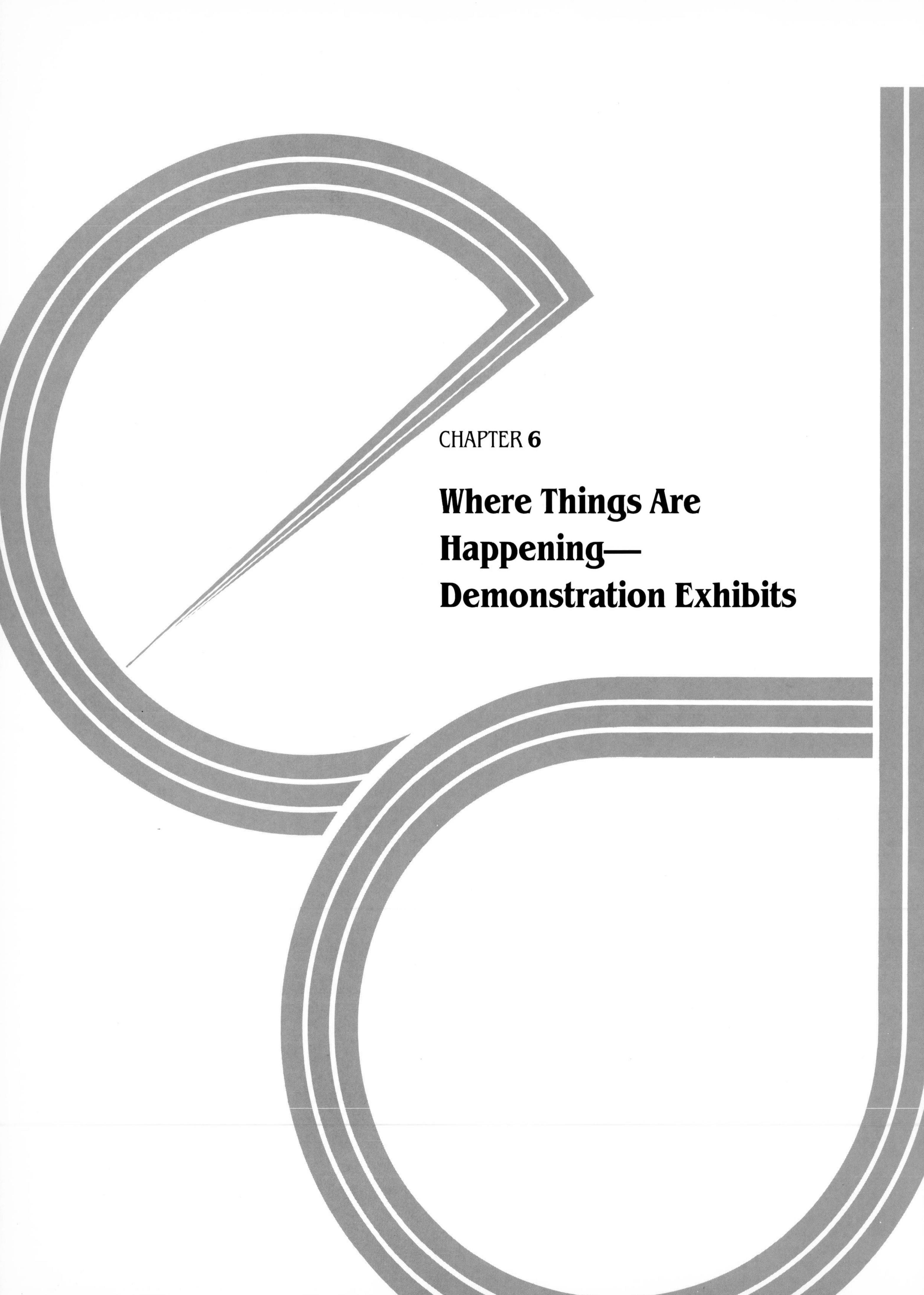

CHAPTER **6**

Where Things Are Happening—Demonstration Exhibits

One of the special characteristics of an exhibit is its potential for actual product presentation. Research studies indicate that the presence of a demonstration is one of the major factors in building memorability. Little wonder, then, that a high proportion of exhibits includes an opportunity for the visitor to see a product or piece of equipment at work, sometimes supported by professional performances.

Wherever possible, then, the designer tries to build in an opportunity for action related to the product in use, and preferably the opportunity for a hands-on approach by the visitor.

Demonstrations, especially when they are one on one, are often placed on the edges of the display area, in order to better attract the casual passerby. This leads to some problems, especially if the demonstration is successful in attracting crowds. Observers begin to pile up, and if the demonstration area is along the aisle, the aisle (and perhaps a neighboring booth) may become blocked. If this happens too often, complaints will probably arise, and the exhibitor may be asked to cease these demonstrations, or at least to move them into the interior of the space.

It is better to think of this at the beginning of the design, and plan it properly. The demonstration should be far enough back to prevent blocking of the aisle, but visible enough from the aisle to attract attention. Most of the time, demonstrations are given whenever a visitor stops and expresses some interest.

More elaborate demonstrations may be given on a schedule. But it is advisable to remember that visitors to a trade show are themselves usually on a schedule. Most of their time will be taken up with visits planned prior to their arrival on the floor, and anything additional is likely to be considered an interruption. Therefore, these performances should be short and frequent. Visitors will rarely stay for a presentation that runs any more than 20 minutes, and even this may be considered too long. Nor will they wait more than 10 or 15 minutes for the next show.

Like one on one demonstrations, these more elaborate ones should be placed so the audience is entirely within the booth space, but the action should be visible to the passerby, to lure him in. The exhibit should be so designed, however, to allow the visitor the option of walking out whenever the urge strikes. Most visitors are reluctant to risk getting into a situation from which they feel they cannot escape.

Occasionally a product story demands more time or greater privacy. In either of these situations, an enclosed presentation area may be desirable. This can be successful, but it needs special handling. It especially needs advance promotion so that the presentation is placed on the prospects' advance schedules. Personalized invitations, scheduled showtimes, and individual tickets are essential factors—the presentation should be considered a major event of the entire trade show.

exhibitor: 20th Century Fox Video
designer: Convention Exhibits, Inc.
producer: Convention Exhibits, Inc.

In a 30 × 50 foot (9 × 15 meter) space, the designer succeeded in getting four spacious conference rooms and 12 operating monitors in a four way walk through exhibit.

exhibitor: Exxon Office Systems
designer: Dirk Haas
producer: Giltspur Exhibits/Rochester

The major demonstration, given by professionals, was given in the central area, enclosed but not blocked off by smoked plexiglass panels. Individual hands on demonstrations were given in three other areas.

Operating microwave ovens were the primary demonstration feature of this exhibit. Also, sinks were installed to show the ease of washing a new line of cookware. A second story conference area was used for private meetings.

exhibitor: Rubbermaid, Inc.
designer: Mike Rowan
producer: Dimensional Media Group II

Racal-Milgo
RACAL
High Speed Modems
Data Encryption
Digitized Voice
Multiplexers
Challenge of the 80's
Racal-Milgo
RACAL
The Electronics Group
Racal-Milgo
Racal-Milgo
Racal-Milgo
Communication
Management
Challenge of the 8
Racal-Milgo
RACAL
The Electronics Group

exhibitor: Racal-Milgo
designers: Bart Peluso/Richard Atwood
producer: Presentations South

A system of 10 foot (3 meter) modules permitted this exhibitor to use a variety of space configurations. Each module was itself a modular, with shelves, light boxes, and graphics all being interchangeable. The special demonstration area was considered the highlight of the exhibit. Scale models of the modules were used for planning.

exhibitor: Mattel Electronics
designer: Fred Calabrese
producer: Exhibit Graphics, Inc.

It was important to permit as many visitors as possible to have hands on experience with the available games. The computer division, however, needed a little more protected area and was given a corner of its own.

MATTEL ELECTRONICS
INTELLIVISION Intelligent Television

INTELLIVISION ENTERTAINMENT COMPUTER SYSTEM

MATTEL ELECTRONICS
AQUARIUS

exhibitor: Pfizer Medical Systems
designers: Ralph Holker/Geoffrey Grieb
producer: Holker & Barry, Inc.

The canopies, whose design was based on elements of the equipment on display, served to cut down the ambient light, especially on the rear illuminated scans.

exhibitor: Ayerst Laboratories
designers: Ralph Holker/Peter Davidson
producer: Holker & Barry, Inc.

This eight foot (2.5 meter) high sculpture, depicting a section through the heart, demonstrates, using fiber optics, polar-motion, and light-emitting diodes, the action of a beta-blocking drug. The action is cued to a recorded narration. Four manned stations permit the booth personnel to detail the physicians.

exhibitor: Ortho Pharmaceutical Corp.
designer: Dimensional Communications, Inc.
producer: Dimensional Communications, Inc.

The slot machines showed products instead of the normal cherries, lemons, and other symbols. Visitors were given prizes as the machines indicated.

exhibitor: Hospital Corporation of America
designers: Clifton B. Rockwood/Janis Osbon
producer: Exhibit 4, Inc.

Designed for the 1982 World's Fair in Knoxville, Tennessee, this exhibit used five talking computers to quiz visitors on their knowledge of health care.

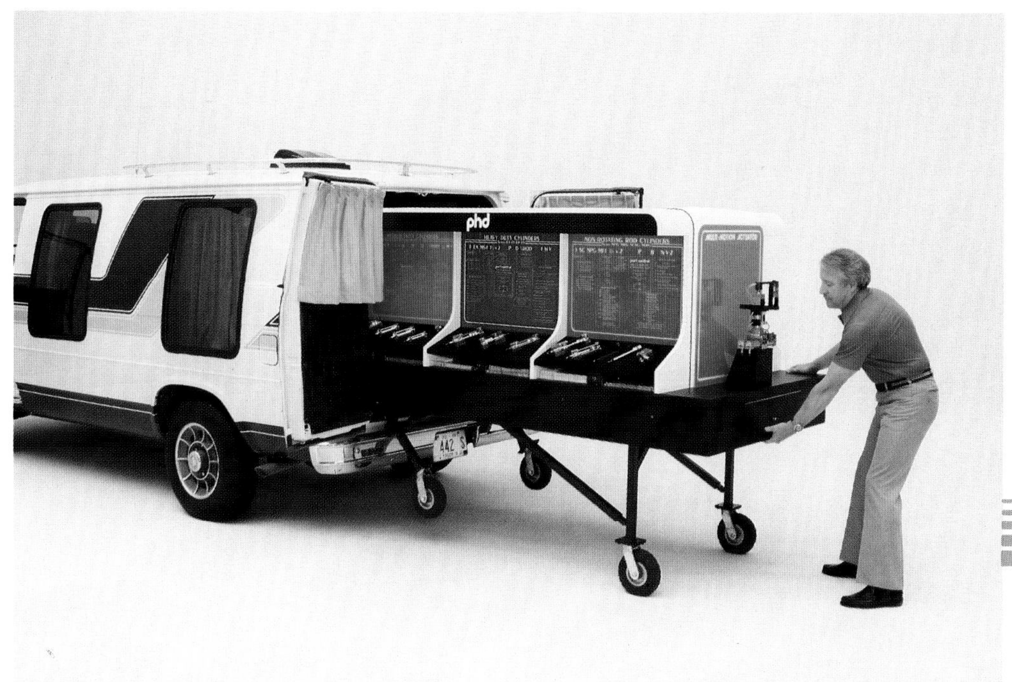

exhibitor: PHD
designer: Pamela K. Smyser
producer: Customcraft

In less than 400 square feet (37 square meters), this highly mobile unit was able to demonstrate working robotic components.

exhibitor: Sandoz Pharmaceuticals
designers: Ralph Holker/Geoffrey Grieb
producer: Holker & Barry, Inc.

The center of this exhibit is a 35 seat theater in which regularly scheduled presentations, promoted in advance, were given by invitation. The tinted plexiglass panels kept the theater separate but not isolated.

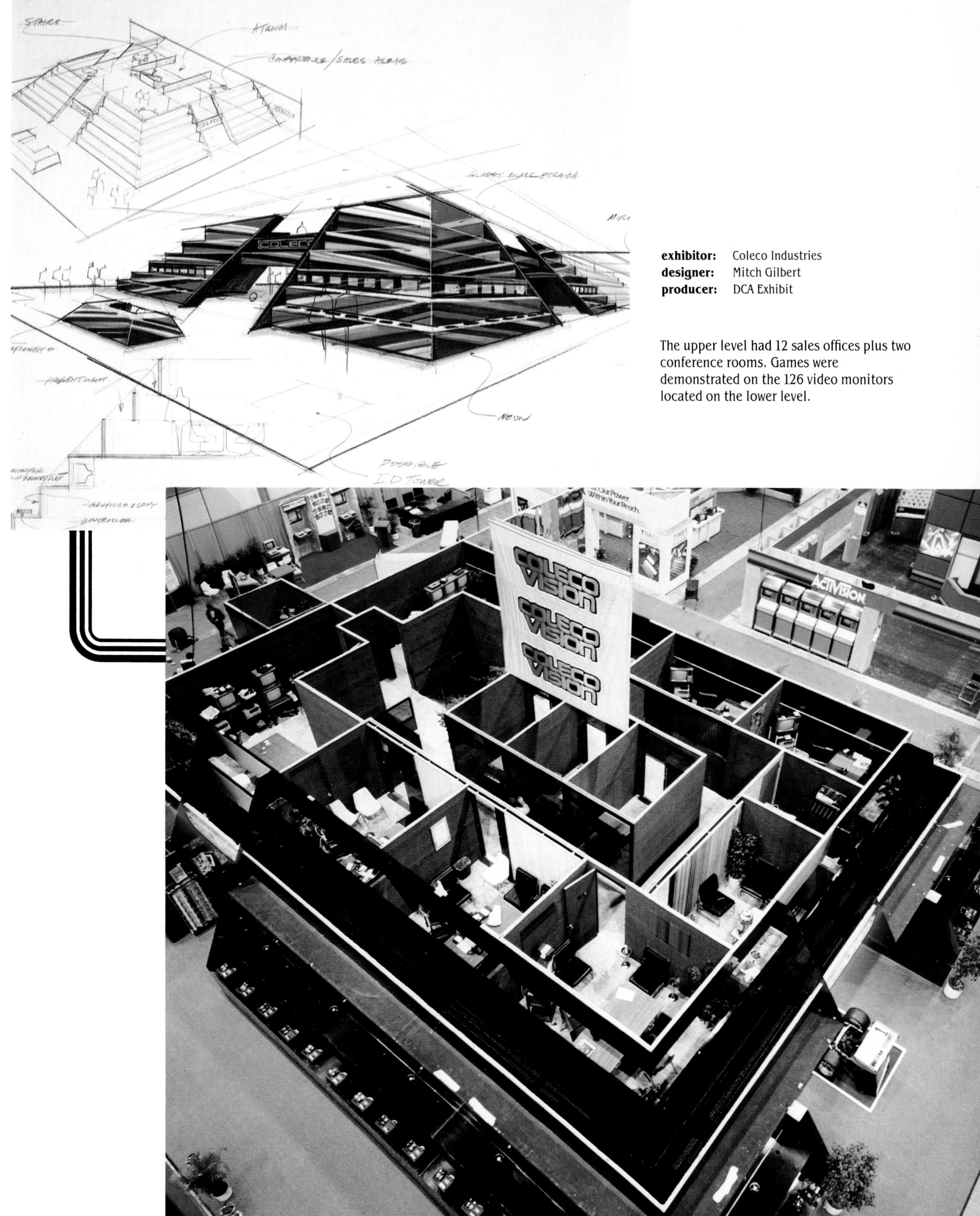

exhibitor: Coleco Industries
designer: Mitch Gilbert
producer: DCA Exhibit

The upper level had 12 sales offices plus two conference rooms. Games were demonstrated on the 126 video monitors located on the lower level.

TERADYNE
TERADYNE
TERADYNE
TERADYNE
BOARD TEST SYSTEM

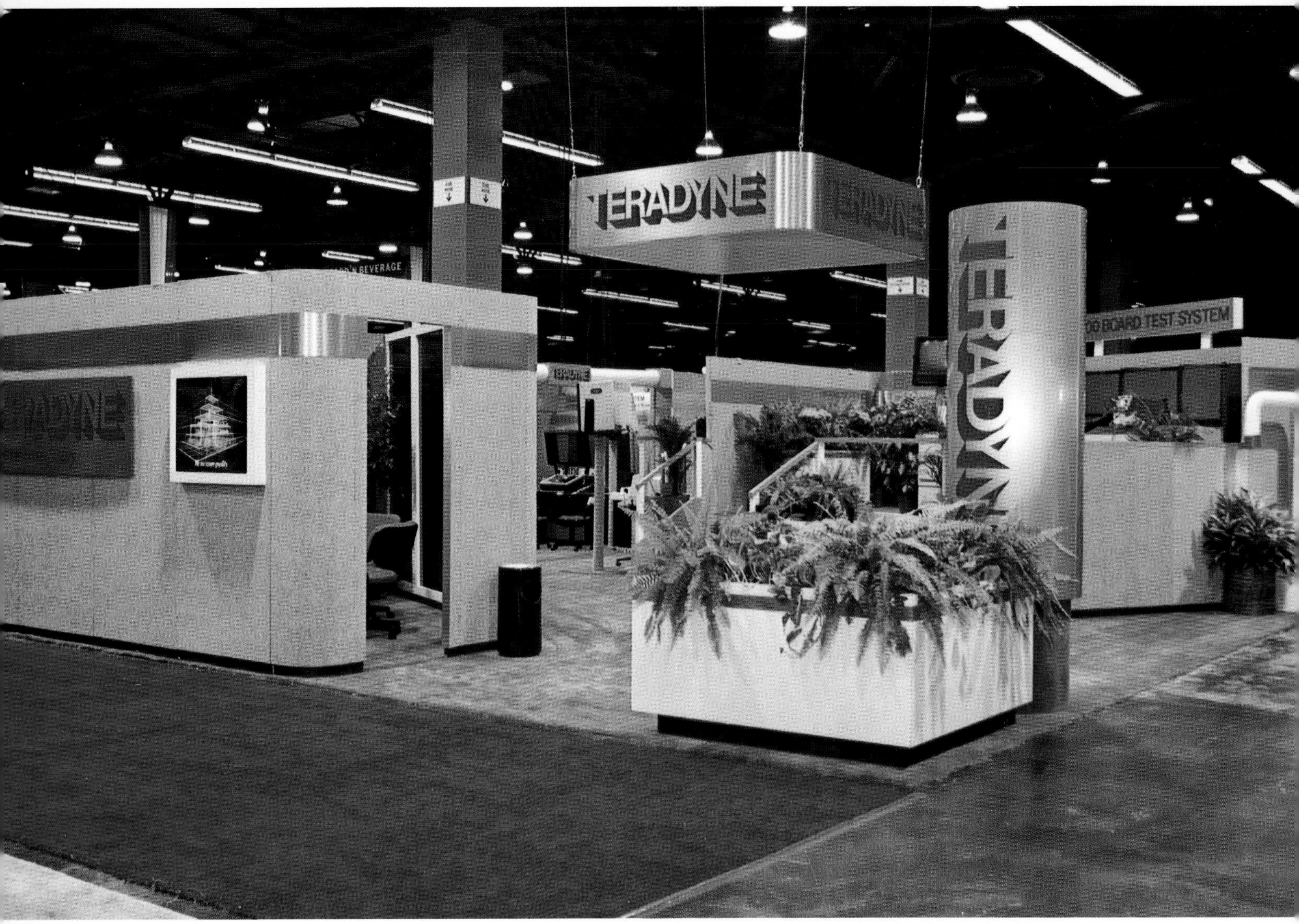

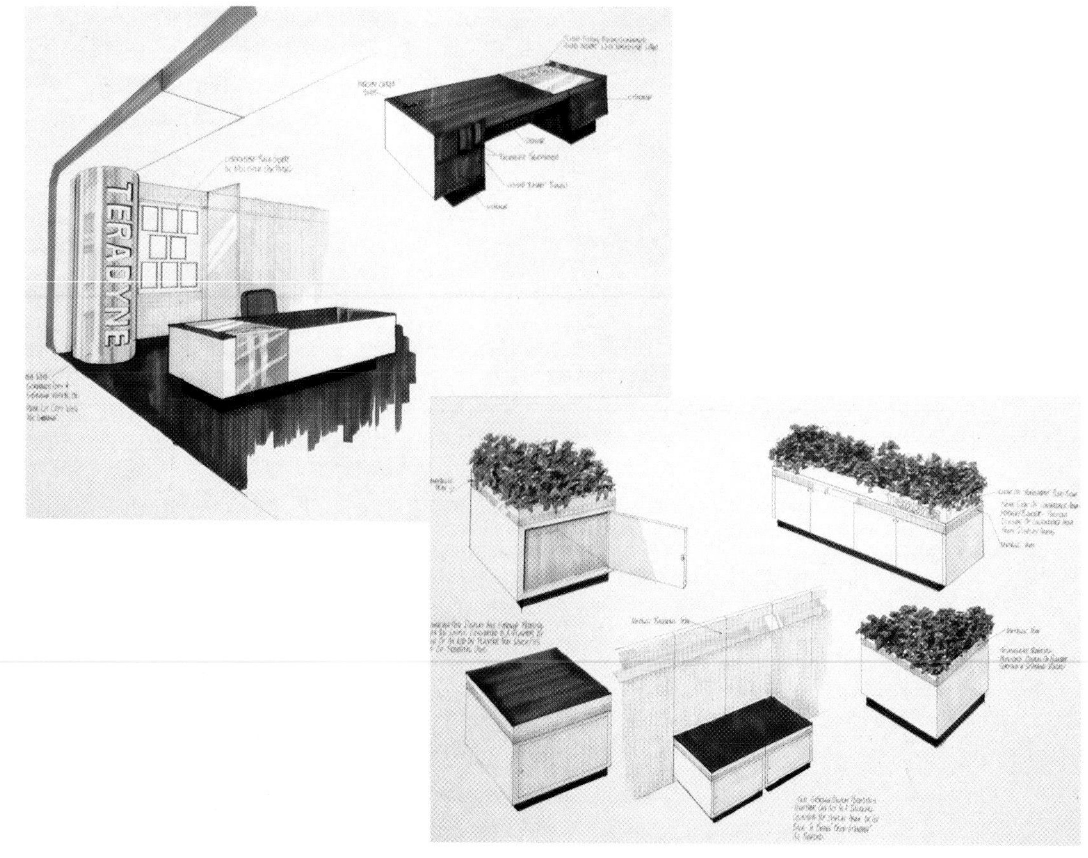

TERADYNE

exhibitor: Teradyne, Inc.
designer: Robert Segal
producer: Fahey Exhibits

While the overall design was open and welcoming, placing the key equipment on a two foot (240 cm) stage acted as a psychological inhibitor to the close inspection by competitors.

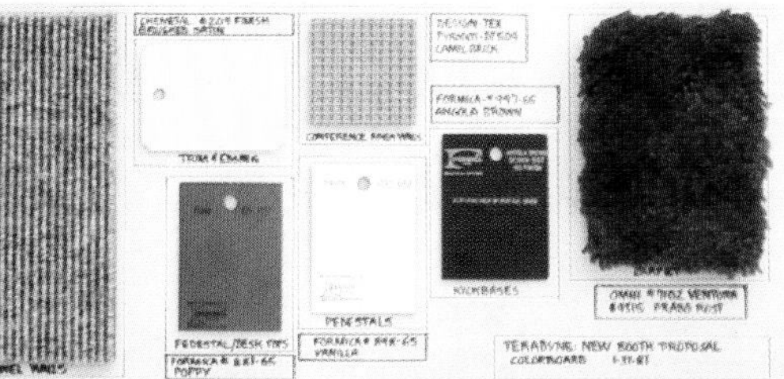

exhibitor: American Hoist & Derrick Co.
designer: Ken Yost
producer: Heritage Communications of St. Paul

When the equipment you want to demonstrate is too big to bring into a convention hall for a demonstration, a working scale model is not only a good substitute but is often more effective than the full scale machine.

exhibitor: Alcan Aluminum Corporation
designer: Robert Albitz
producer: George P. Johnson Co.

The highlight of this exhibit, with its 30 × 42 foot (9 × 13 meter) canopy, was a central demonstration area, under a 16 × 16 foot (5 × 5 meter) inner canopy. On a 14 foot (4 meter) turntable was a one half scale model car of clear plastic. Above it was an eight sided gondola which contained four video monitors. Product display modules were placed at the four corners of the exhibit.

exhibitor: Braun Canada Ltd.
designer: A. Harrison
producer: Kadoke Display Ltd.

A long counter area permitted easy demonstration of one or more of the appliances displayed on the shelves along the back wall.

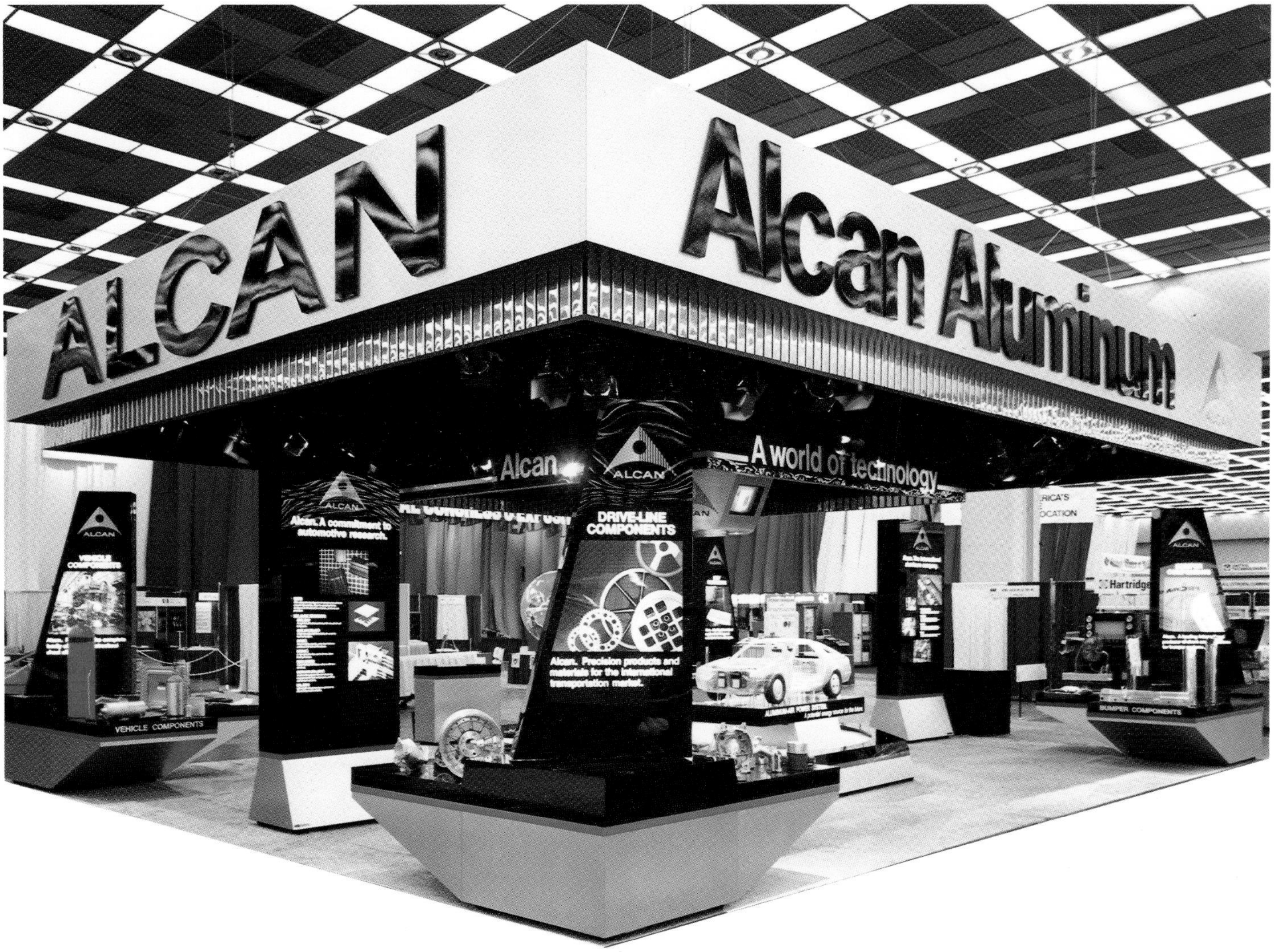
ALCAN
Alcan Aluminum
Alcan
A world of technology
DRIVE-LINE COMPONENTS
Alcan. Precision products and materials for the international transportation market.
Alcan. A commitment to automotive research.
VEHICLE COMPONENTS
BUMPER COMPONENTS
Hartridge

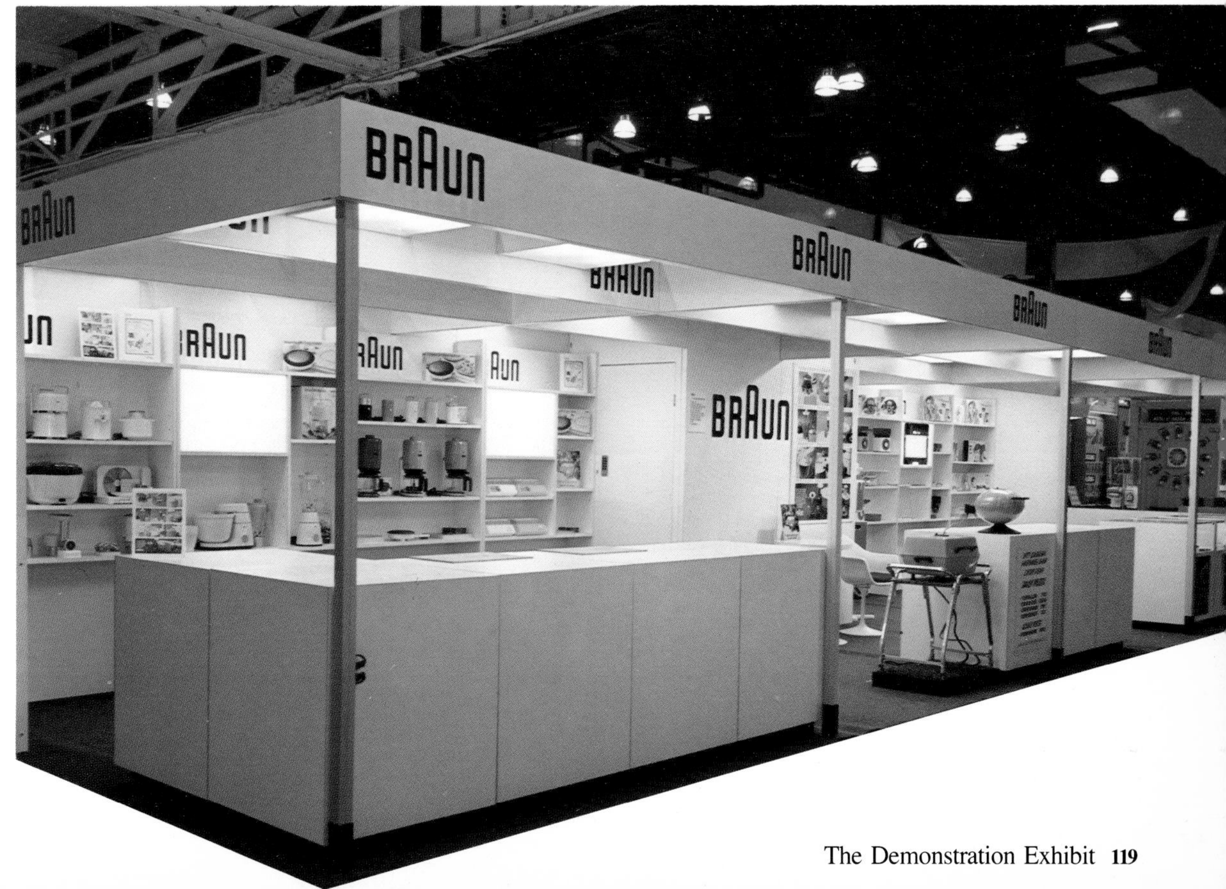

BRAUN
BRAUN
BRAUN
BRAUN

exhibitor: Black & Decker (U.S.), Inc.
designer: Mike Rowan
producer: Cyclonics

The first stage in the development of an exhibit is usually a drawing or color rendering.

exhibitor: Black & Decker (U.S.), Inc.
designer: Martin Spicuzzi
producer: Cyclonics

In exhibiting hand tools, it is possible to use small demonstration areas which can be placed at various points in a larger area.

NEW
NEW
Workmate Accessories
from Black & Decker
B&D

Black & Decker
Black & Decker
B&D

B&D
Black & Decker
Black & Decker
Black & Decker
the new products
company

INA

exhibitor: INA Bearings
designer: General Exhibits, Inc.
producer: General Exhibits, Inc.

To illustrate the role of bearings in automobiles, a full size car of the future was constructed of smoked plexiglass. Each bearing was painted in a fluorescent color and illuminated with black light. As the narration went on, synchronized signals turned on the appropriate light.

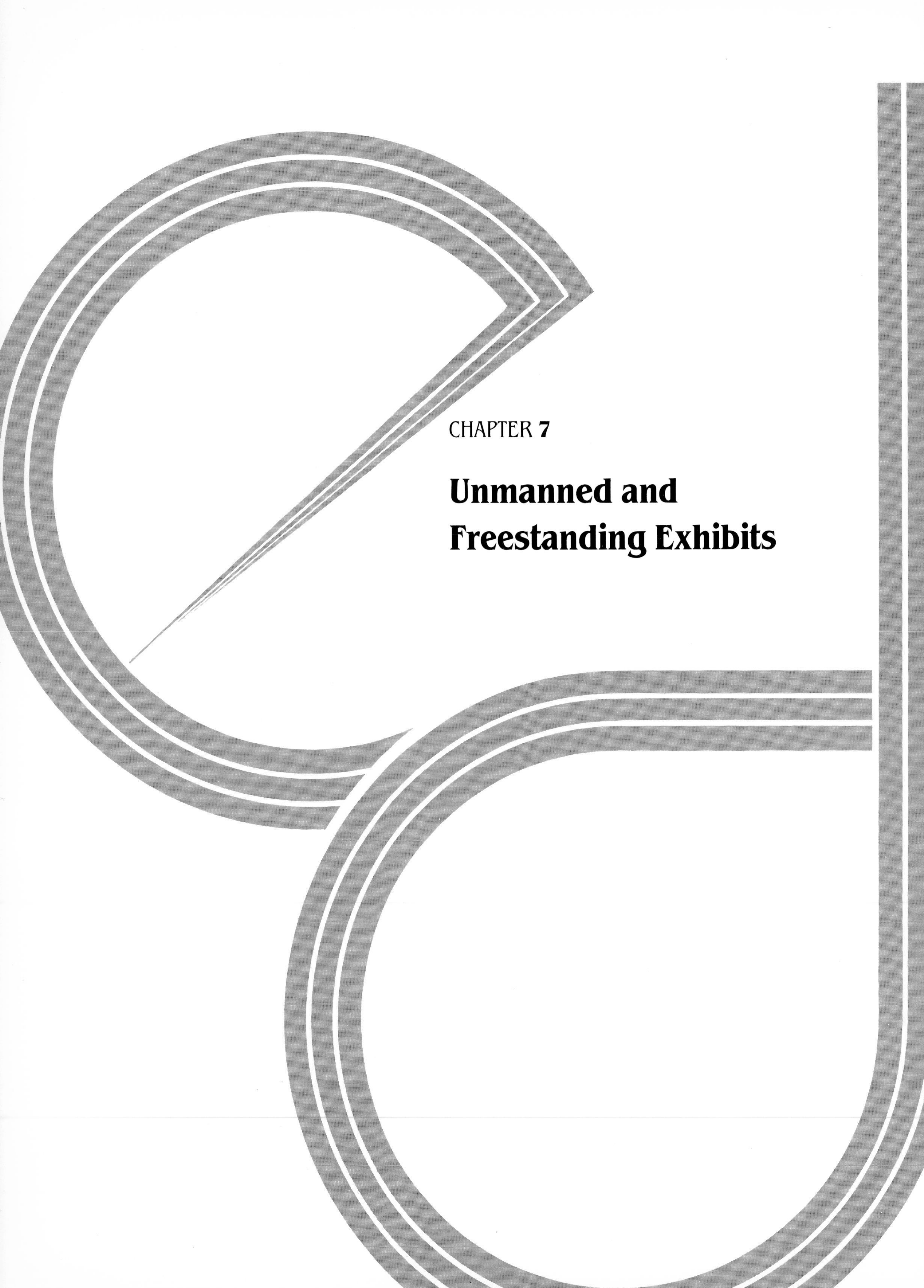

CHAPTER **7**

Unmanned and Freestanding Exhibits

Most of the exhibits shown in this book are intended to be used in trade shows, where they essentially serve as a back-up, or perhaps nothing more than a background, for sales personnel of the exhibiting company. They furnish exhibitor personnel with an environment in which they can function. In addition, they are designed to appear in a competitive situation, in which many exhibitors are trying to attract prospects to themselves and away from other exhibitors.

This chapter, in contrast, consists of exhibits which do not have the assistance of booth personnel; while their purpose is certainly to attract attention, they are not in competition with other booths. Their competition is the world as a whole.

Such exhibits are found in building lobbies, showrooms, shopping malls and centers, and also at trade shows. Their location may limit their potential audience to a specific group, like employees of a single company, or they may appeal to a broader audience, like people who walk through a shopping mall.

While exhibits of this type superficially resemble trade show exhibits, they are necessarily more self-contained.

Many of the exhibits seen in this chapter utilize ready-made systems or components. This option is often less costly and allows the exhibitor to arrange his or her display in various configurations. This makes these exhibits very popular among exhibitors. In some respects, the exhibitor can become his or her own designer. With custom kits from manufacturers, an exhibitor can construct and design an exhibit to his or her specific needs—gearing it toward the audience that needs to be reached. This is important since these exhibits must create attention without the use of personnel. Also, easily changed graphics make it simple to alter the direction of an exhibit—at a cost and time savings.

Another advantage of this style of exhibit is its portability. Many of the ready-made systems and kits come complete with their own carrying case. After the show, the exhibit is folded up, packed into the case, and carried away by a single person. Storage, transportation, set up, and take down are all accomplished in very little time at very little cost. A definite plus for any exhibitor.

exhibitor: Home Box Office
designer: Tom LaGreca/Etta Siegel
producer: Extraversion

Home Box Office utilized this multi-paneled exhibit to display its many special programs of the past decade. The exhibit could be set up in different configurations and changed easily just by adding different panels. This exhibit was for the Museum of Broadcasting Show.

exhibitor: Psychiatric Institute of America
designer: Jocelyn Voros
producer: Joan Carol Associates

With many different types of target audiences, this exhibitor needed the ability to alter the direction and appearance of the display.

exhibitor: The National Guard
designer: Needham, Harper & Steers
producer: Outline by Extraversion

This unit, which folded into a canvas carrying case, could be easily carried to any location. Another advantage of the system was the easily changeable graphics.

Coke is it!
For Real Taste.
Enjoy
Coke
Enjoy
Coca-Cola
Drink
ICE COLD
Coca-Cola
SOLD HERE
Coca-Cola
TIME
Drink
Coca-Cola
What Happened in Atlanta
ANNUAL REPORT
GOING UP
Coke is it!
For Real Taste.

exhibitor: The Coca-Cola Company
designer: Ezra Wittner
producer: Sugar Creek Exhibits, Inc.

This traveling exhibit promoted the exhibitor's tie in with the USA Olympic Hall of Fame. The five circular islands displayed memorabilia of past olympic stars, with captions on the acrylic stands and banners bearing the exhibitor's logo above the islands. Intended for shopping mall use, the exhibit traveled in a custom fitted truck.

exhibitor: The Coca-Cola Company
designer: Jim Walker
producer: Walker Studios

This exhibit, in the corporate lobby, shows more than 400 articles from the corporation's archives.

exhibitor: Holy Cross Hospital
designer: M. Drue Gillis
producer: Shotel, Inc.

This exhibit was designed for installation in a public area of the hospital, thereby minimizing the need for sponsor identification.

exhibitor: CBI Industries
producer: Technical Exhibits

The Connectra System from Technical Exhibits, Inc. is used in this exhibit.

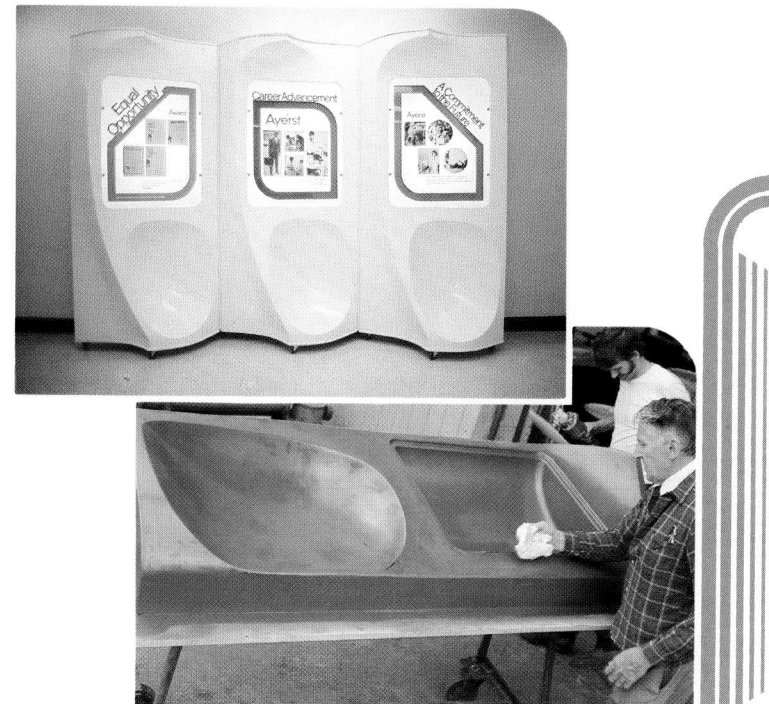

exhibitor: Ayerst Laboratories
designers: Ralph Holker/R. Alexander
producer: Holker & Barry, Inc.

Made of molded plastic, these flexible units are rigid and lightweight, with easily changed back-lit graphics.

exhibitor: Lockheed Aircraft/TWA
designer: J. Lynn Hickman
producer: Walter E. Zemitzsch, Inc.

In an effort to be as innovative and futuristic as the new TriStar aircraft itself, this exhibit used compound angled pylons projecting upward and outward from a star-shaped base. The illuminated transparency boxes were designed to suggest aircraft windows. This award-winning design is currently on exhibit in Paris.

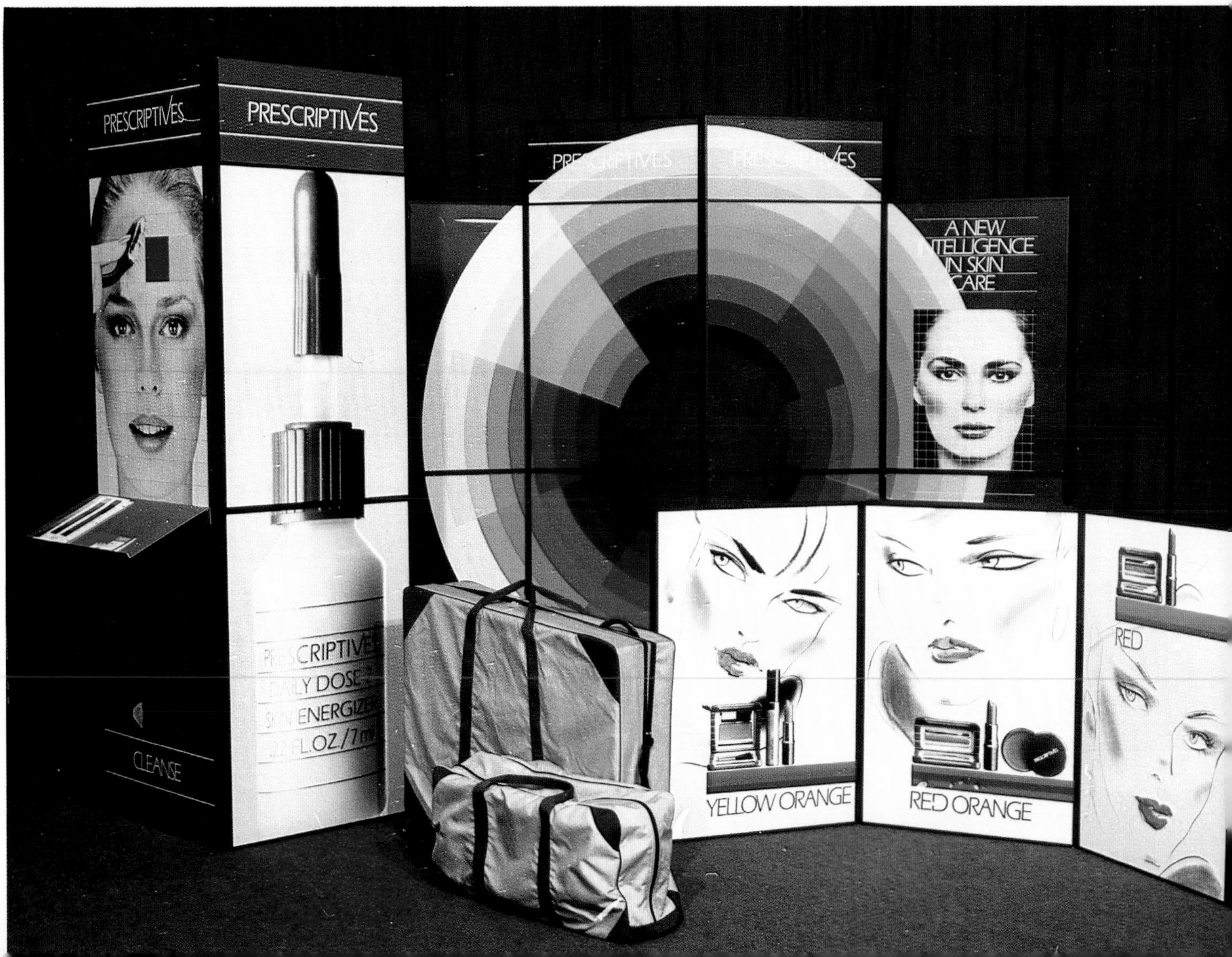

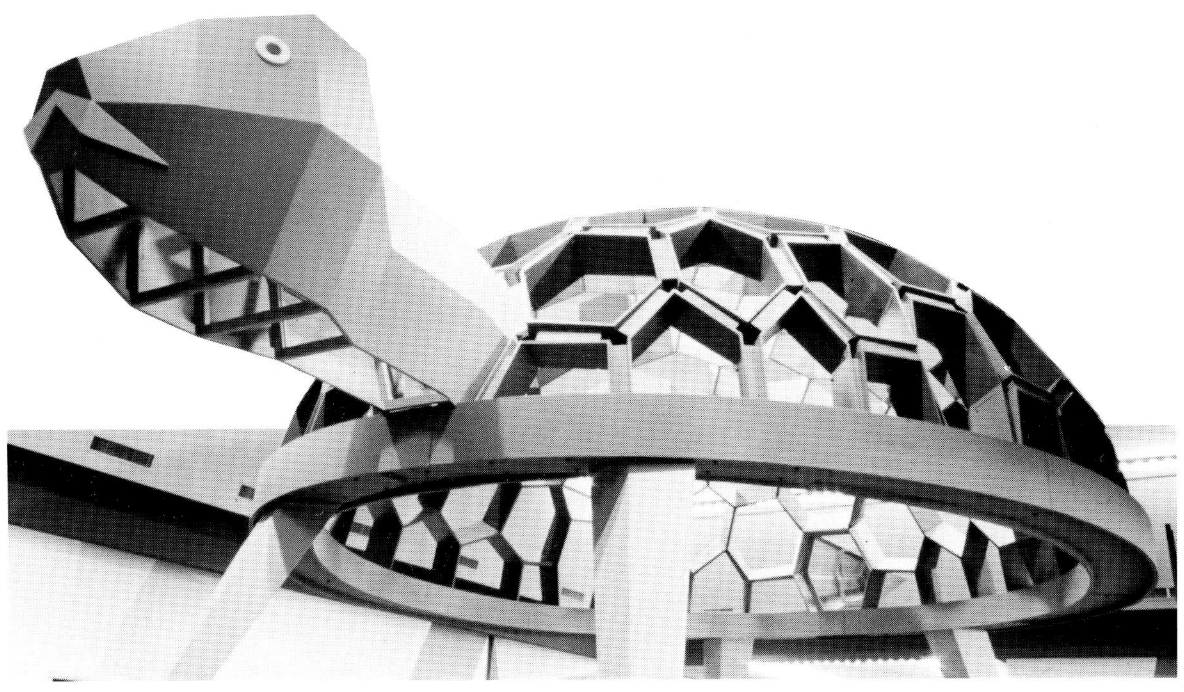

exhibitor: Cedonial Mall/Baltimore
designer: General Exhibits, Inc.
producer: General Exhibits, Inc.

In one of its most unusual projects produced over its 50 year history, General Exhibits of Philadelphia designed and constructed this 60 foot (18 meter) long, 30 foot (9 meter) high, 20,000 pound (9,072 kilogram) turtle for a shopping center near Baltimore.

exhibitor: Estee Lauder
designers: Estee Lauder/Outline by Extraversion
producer: Outline by Extraversion

These flexible units, which could use different graphic materials for different marketing situations, were used for selling outposts in department stores.

The Gelatin Dry Plate Process
The Gelatin Dry Plate Process
6.
7.
The Early Darkroom
Flexible Film

The Early Darkroom
4.
Panoramic and Stereoscopic Photography
3.
The Wet Plate Process

exhibitor: Eastman Kodak Company
designer: Exhibitgroup Chicago
producer: Exhibitgroup Chicago

This historical exhibit featured photographic artifacts from the Kodak Patent Museum, the George Eastman House, and from private collections.

exhibitor: Biedenharn Museum—Vicksburg, Mississippi
designer: Jim Walker
producer: Walker Studio

In 1894, in this room Joseph Biedenharn made his first commercial bottling of Coca-Cola. Backed by a contemporary photograph of the waterfront of Vicksburg, the first cases depict the origins of the exhibitor, with authentic replicas of early bottling equipment, followed by photographs giving the history of the community, interspersed with events from the life of the company.

Located adjacent to the main corporate conference room, this is essentially a chronological display of marketing materials used by the company through the years. The exhibit begins with an 1886 dispenser and ends with a digital read-out that counts each day's consumption of Coca-Cola and gives an accumulative number for the year's consumption worldwide.

exhibitor: The Coca-Cola Company
designer: Bob Naas
producer: Walker Studio

VICKSBURG 1894

Coca-Cola
Coke Quality Remains as Times Change

The design of this exhibit was based on the exhibitor's name. Each letter stood about eight feet (two and one-half meters) high and contained a segment of information about the exhibitor. Most of the letters had light boxes, but one had a video rear screen.

exhibitor: Commline, a division of Cox Cable Communications
designer: Ezra Wittner
producer: Sugar Creek Exhibits, Inc.

exhibitor: AT&T
designer: Eugene De Christopher
producer: Exhibitgroup San Francisco

A permanent installation, this display features a tunnel and an audiovisual theater that uses mirrors on the interior to reflect the images being projected from the wall directly in front of the entry way.

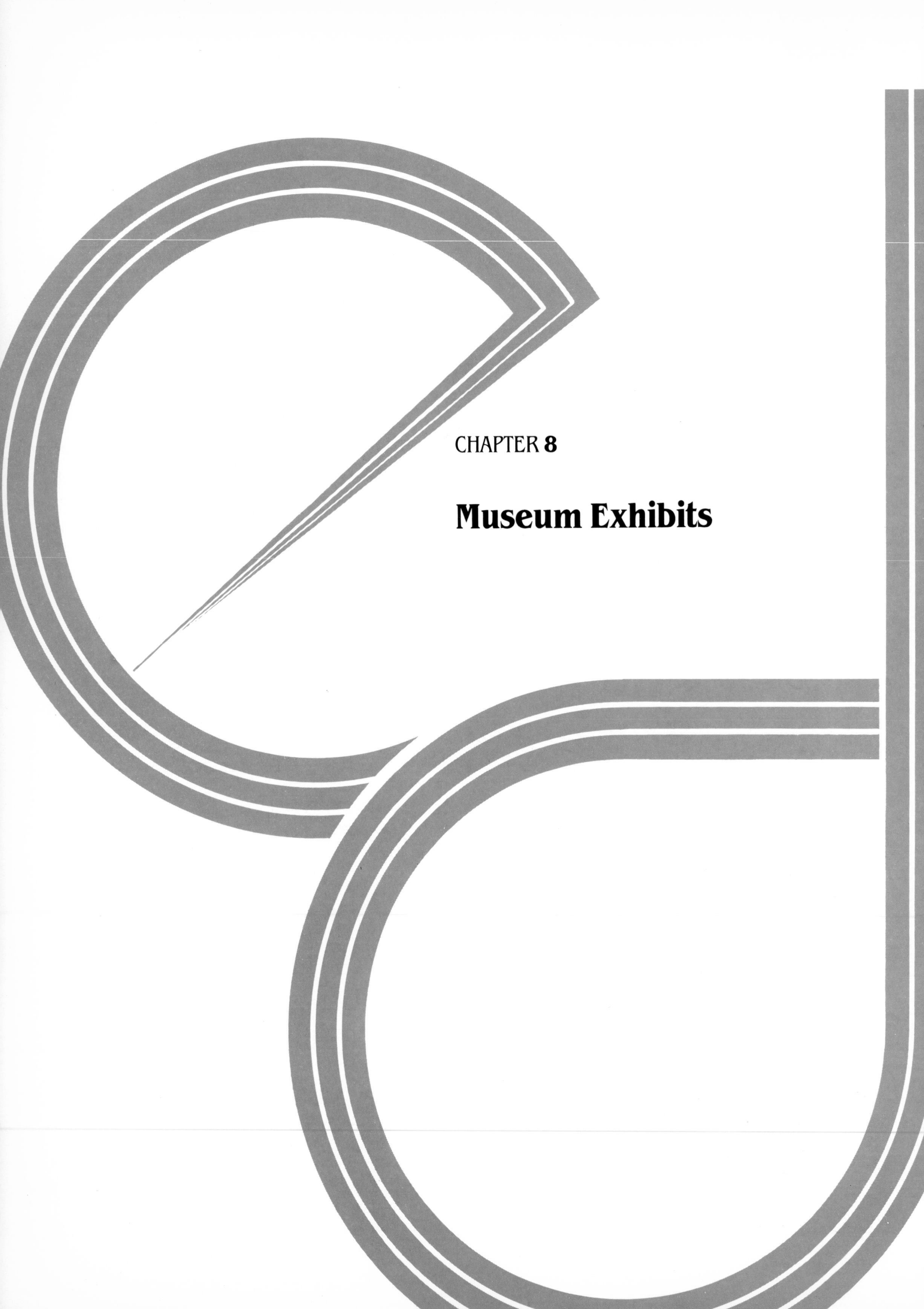

CHAPTER **8**

Museum Exhibits

The museum is an important part of the exhibit world, but it must be considered separately from the trade show exhibit. Not only does it differ in purpose, but the physical requirements, and the entire approach that it necessitates, are quite different.

The most obvious distinction between the museum and the trade show exhibit is that of permanence. While nothing in today's culture can be called permanent, most museum exhibits are designed to remain in place for a year or more. Even traveling exhibits will stay put for several weeks before moving on to another city. On the other hand, trade show exhibits are often designed for a single major show lasting a week at most, and even those destined for reuse usually have to be prepared for changing exhibit hall configurations; graphics may also be changed for each show.

A trade show exhibit, on the whole, is designed as a background for booth personnel. It is intended to serve as an environment for a special kind of selling. Its graphics, its visuals, its demonstration devices are there to supplement the presentation of the salesperson in the booth, and to make the sales pitch more persuasive. The exhibit may or may not work without a salesperson. The museum exhibit, on the other hand, must be self-sufficient. While occasionally there may be a guide or a docent, or even a recorded commentary received on personal earphones, the designer cannot count on this assistance.

Further, a museum exhibit must often provide information on more than one level. One can expect that many visitors, perhaps even a majority, will come into the exhibit area with little real interest or knowledge of the material. They will glance at the displays, read only what is shown in the largest type, and go on. Others may spend a little more time, read subheads as well as heads, and learn a little more. A handful will look at every artifact on display, study all the graphics, read all the captions. A good exhibit design will satisfy visitors at all these levels.

Museum exhibits often lead the way in new exhibit techniques. There is more room for experimentation, and sometimes even more money. This is especially true of exhibits designed for world's fairs. The objectives, the budgets, and the size of the prospective audiences encourage investigation of new ways of communicating. Most world's fairs, like museums, are excellent places for designers to enlarge their horizons.

exhibitor: Department of the Treasury
producer: General Exhibits, Inc.

The story line for this exhibit was based on the development of taxation. The primary technique of presentation was synchronized audio, with theatrical sequential lighting in a series of environmental settings. As the visitor walked from one area to another, he or she automatically activated the appropriate exhibit. The unit was illuminated and the tape commentary started.

REPAY
HE NATIONAL DEBT.
ROTECT AND PROMOTE
NEW INDUSTRY.
ITIATE A FEDERAL
BANKING SYSTEM.
CENTRALIZE
GOVERNMENT
PURCHASING.

exhibitor: Department of the Treasury
producer: General Exhibits, Inc.

This exhibit is based on the history of the U.S. Department of the Treasury. Displays of all sizes and shapes comprise the exhibit which gives a detailed dose of American history.

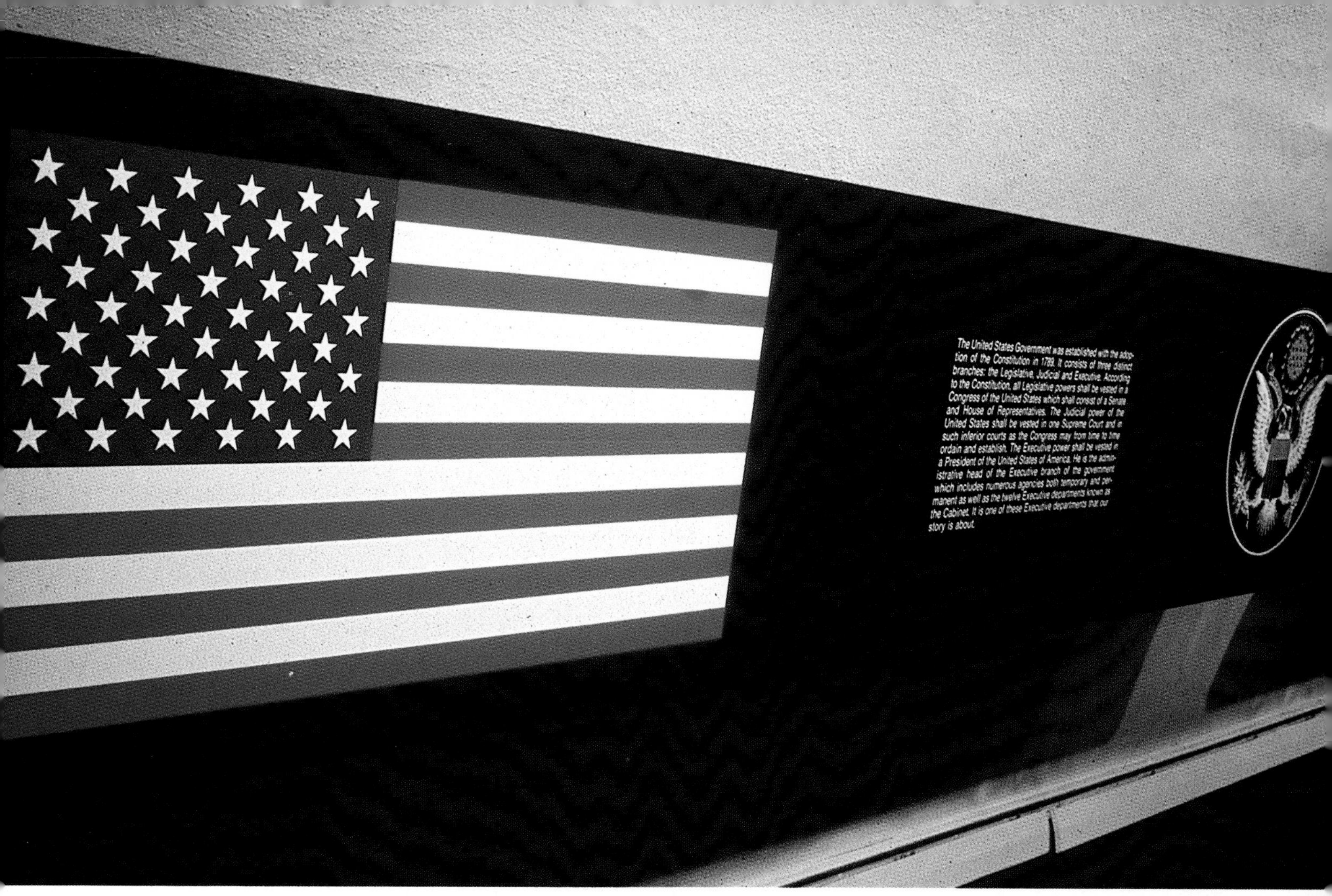

The United States Government was established with the adop-
tion of the Constitution in 1789. It consists of three distinct
branches: the Legislative, Judicial and Executive. According
to the Constitution, all Legislative powers shall be vested in a
Congress of the United States which shall consist of a Senate
and House of Representatives. The Judicial power of the
United States shall be vested in one Supreme Court and in
such inferior courts as the Congress may from time to time
ordain and establish. The Executive power shall be vested in
a President of the United States of America. He is the admin-
istrative head of the Executive branch of the government
which includes numerous agencies both temporary and permanent as well as the twelve Executive departments known as
the Cabinet. It is one of these Executive departments that our
story is about.

exhibitor: State of Alaska Bicentennial
designer: General Exhibits, Inc.
producer: General Exhibits, Inc.

Celebrating Alaska's bicentennial was also a celebration of Alaska's future. This exhibit highlighted the state's various regions and its strengths in industry, education, and natural resources.

Flying for
Alaska's Future
Natural
Resources

federal
state
building
Alaska's
future
industry
city
man

exhibitor: Department of Transportation
designer: General Exhibits, Inc.
producer: General Exhibits, Inc.

This exhibit highlighted the many aspects of transportation, and transportation systems, available in the United States.

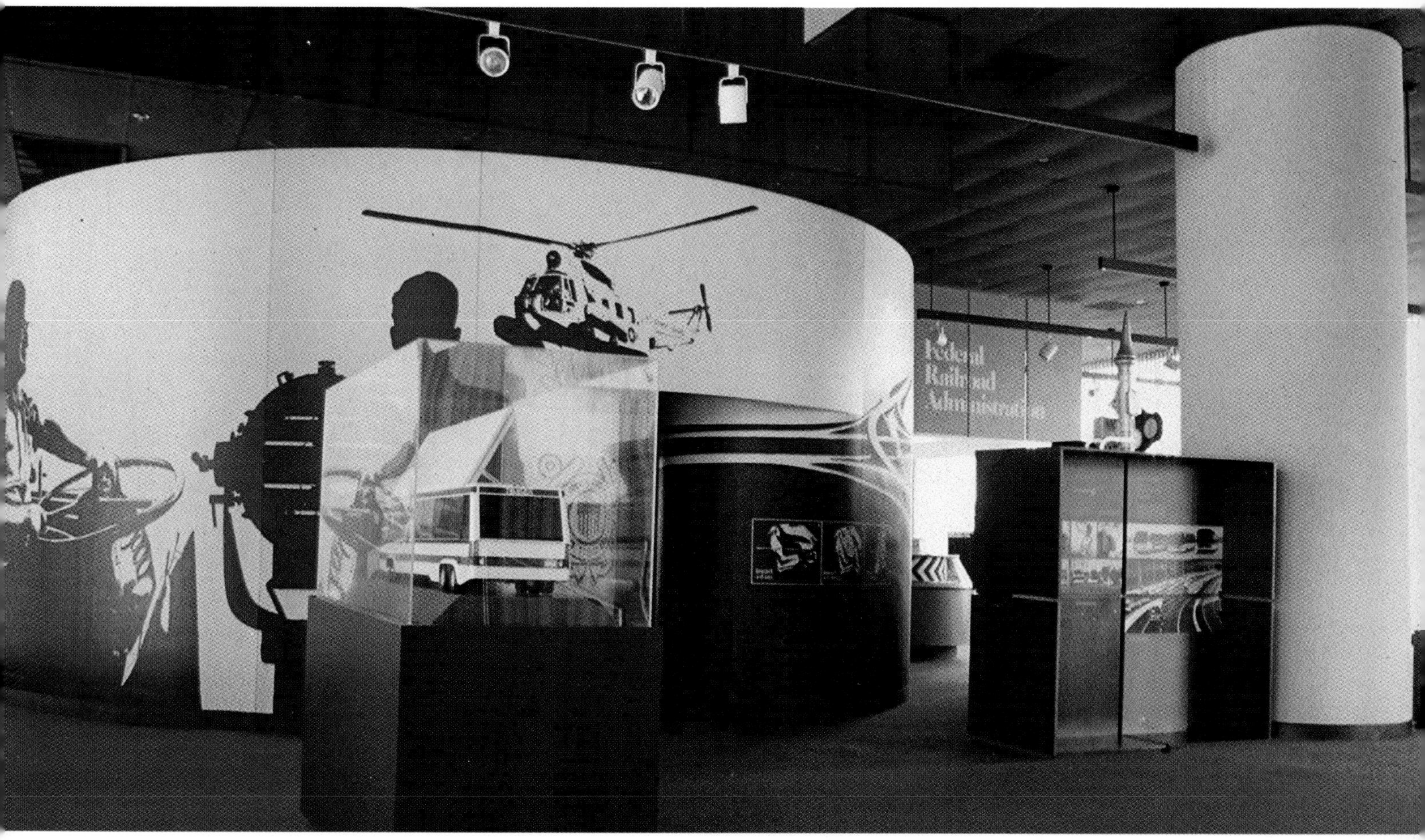
Federal
Railroad
Administration

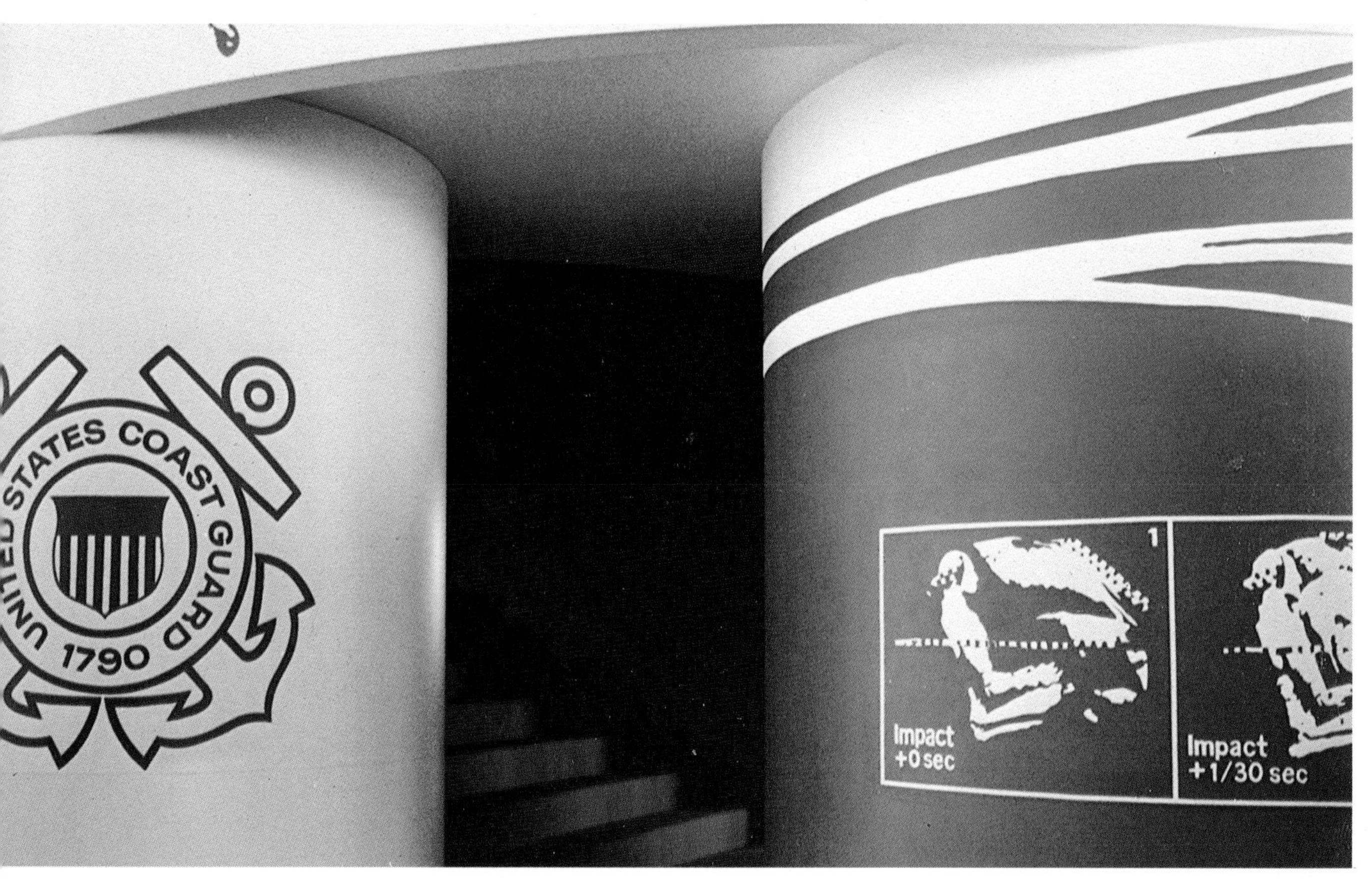

UNITED STATES COAST GUARD
1790
1
Impact
+0 sec
Impact
+1/30 sec

(LEFT) **exhibitor:** Federal Highway Traffic Safety Administration
producer: General Exhibits, Inc.

This exhibit, emphasizing traffic safety and education, used many different colors, shapes, and arrangements in order to attract attention.

(RIGHT) **exhibitor:** Children's Museum—Caracas, Venezuela
designer/producer: General Exhibits and Displays, Inc.

An animated fractioning tower explains how oil is refined.

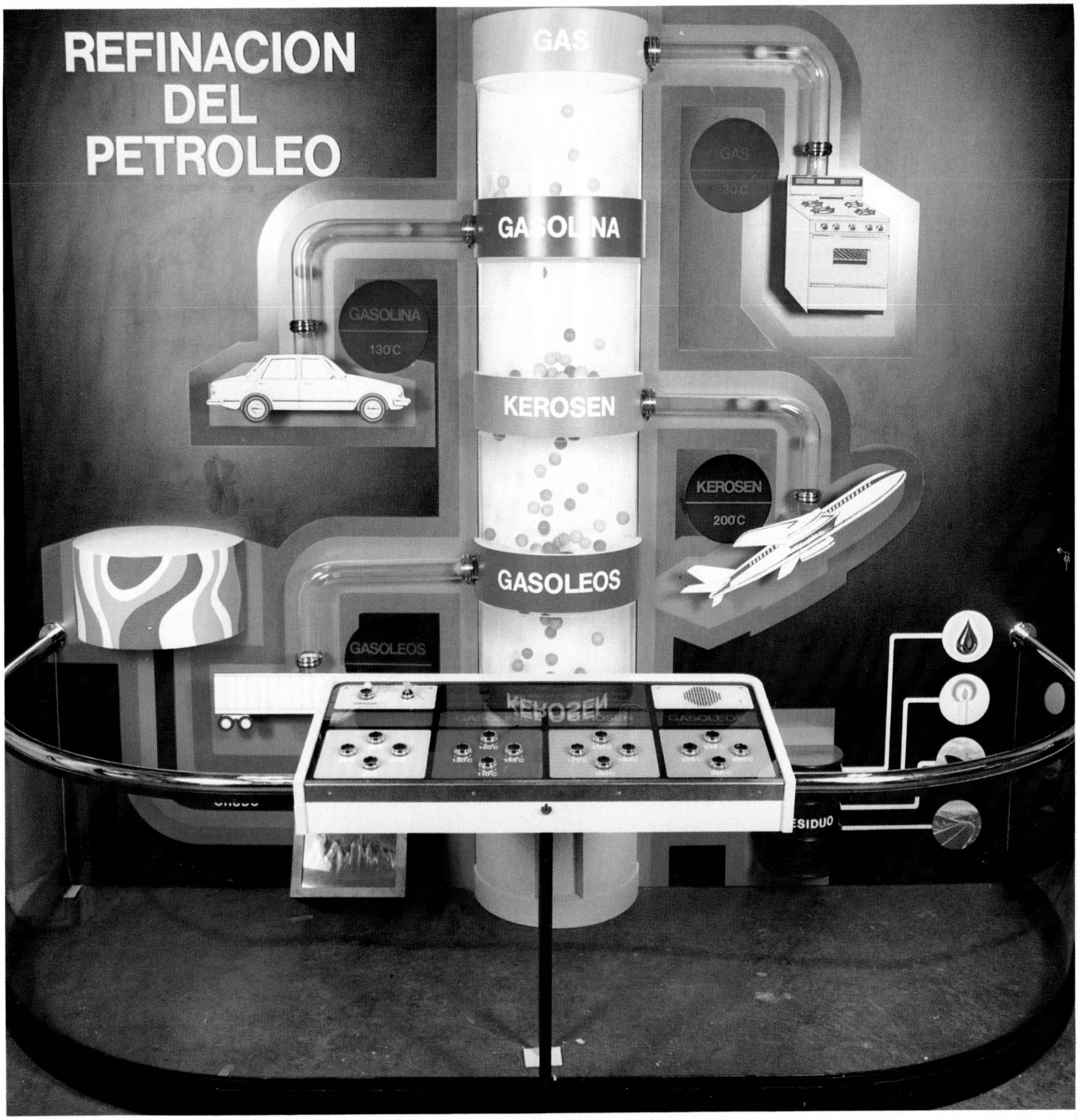

(RIGHT) **exhibitor:** National Air and Space Musuem/Space Hall
producer: General Exhibits, Inc.

As one of the attractions at Space Hall in Washington, D.C., this lifesize exhibit helps to explain one phase of American travel into space.

exhibitor: National Aquarium in Baltimore
designer: C7A
producer: General Exhibits, Inc.

The National Aquarium in Baltimore, Maryland utilizes detailed graphics and actual demonstrations in its exhibits. Every type of aquatic life is highlighted throughout the modern styled building.

"If there is magic on this planet, it is contained in water."

Loren Eiseley

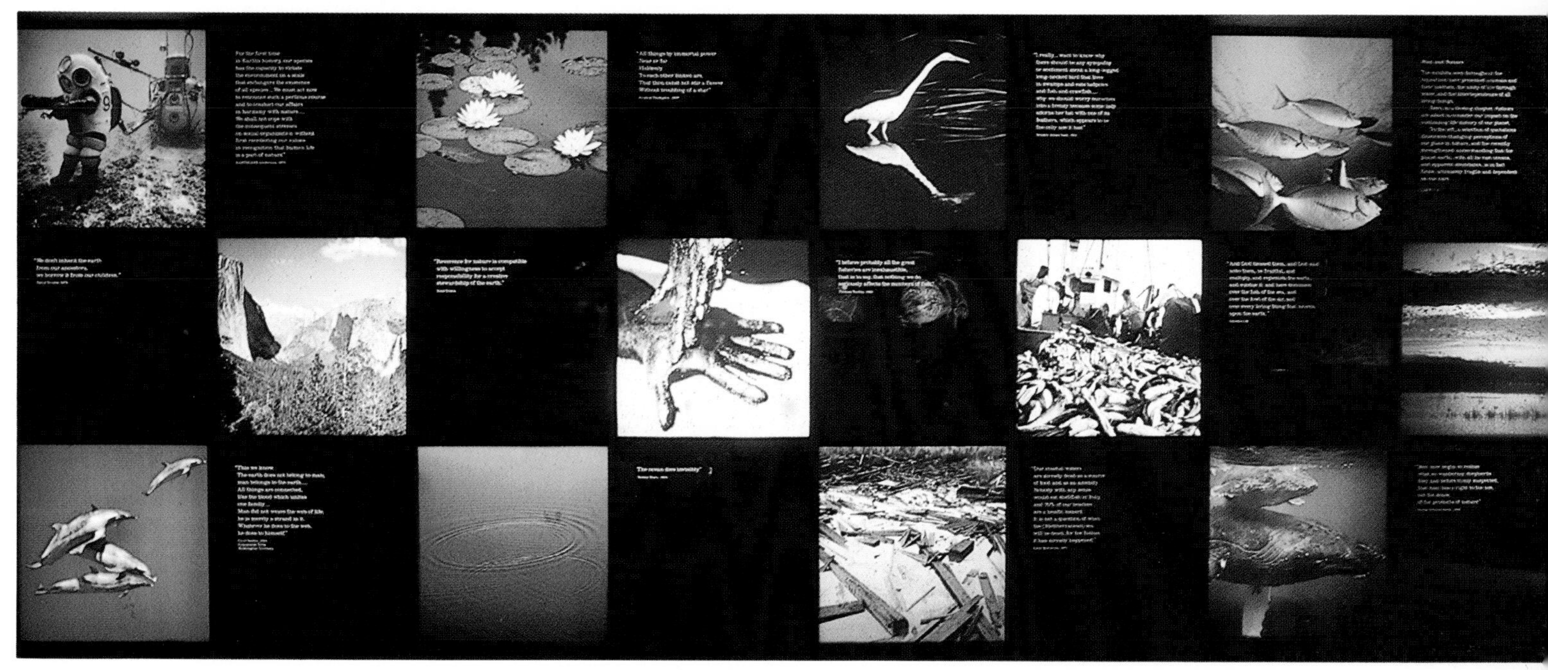

Children's Cove
Out→

exhibitor: National Aquarium in Baltimore
designer: C7A
producer: General Exhibits, Inc.

The exhibits shown here, and others not illustrated, cover five floors of a building on Baltimore's renovated waterfront. While basic design was by the architects, the producer was responsible for all detailing, as well as installation. Silkscreening was used extensively, mostly for identification and directional purposes, as well as stretched transparency murals which were illuminated from the rear. The largest transparency mural was more than 10 feet long.

exhibitor: National Aquarium in Baltimore
designer: C7A
producer: General Exhibits, Inc.

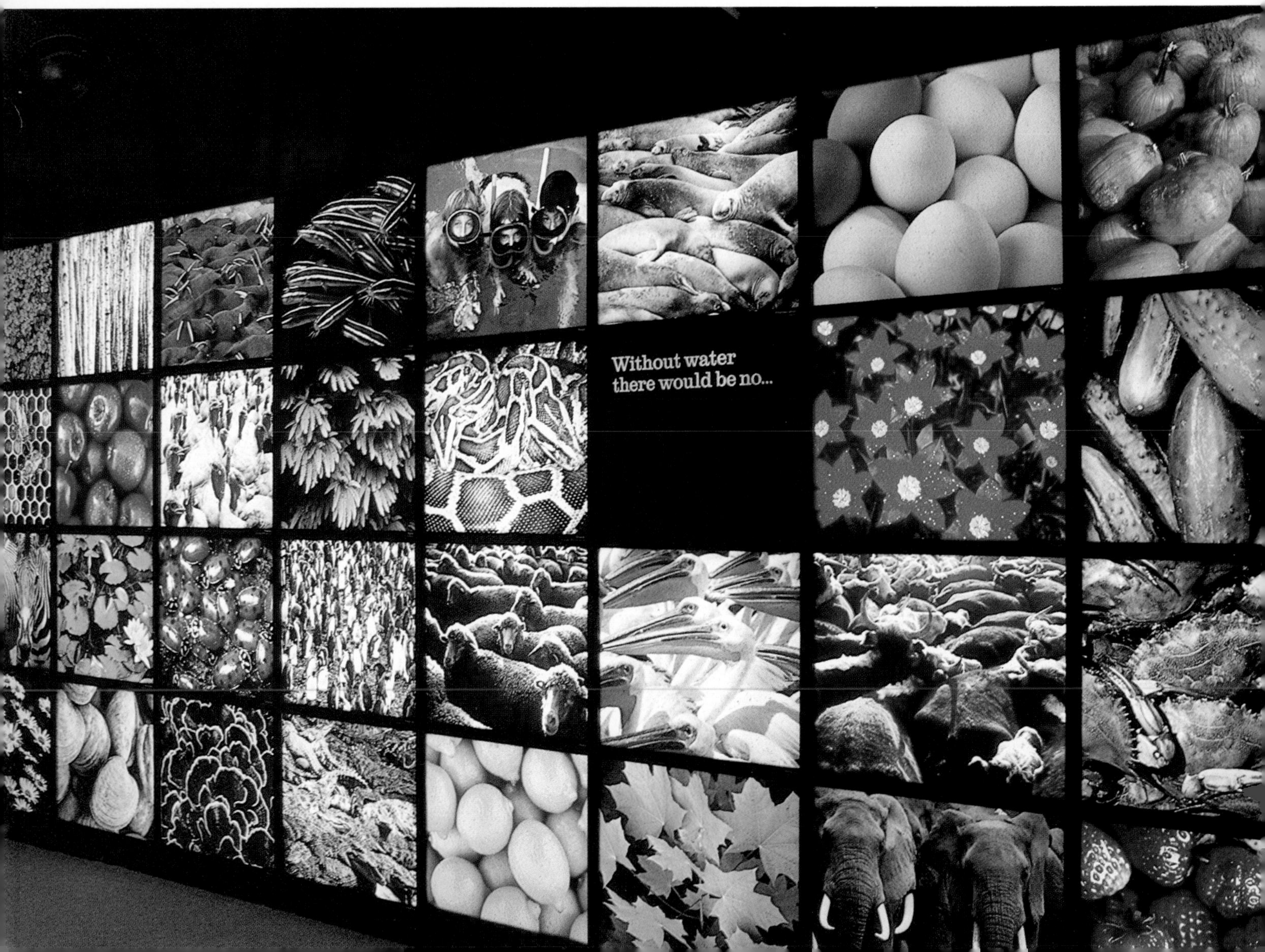

Without water
there would be no...

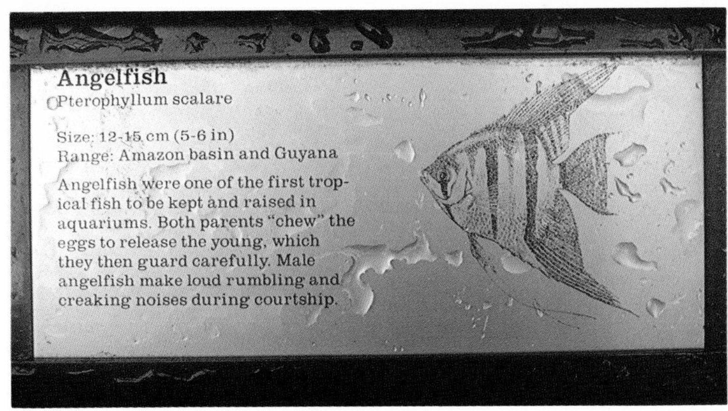
Angelfish
Pterophyllum scalare
Size: 12-15 cm (5-6 in)
Range: Amazon basin and Guyana
Angelfish were one of the first tropical fish to be kept and raised in aquariums. Both parents "chew" the eggs to release the young, which they then guard carefully. Male angelfish make loud rumbling and creaking noises during courtship.

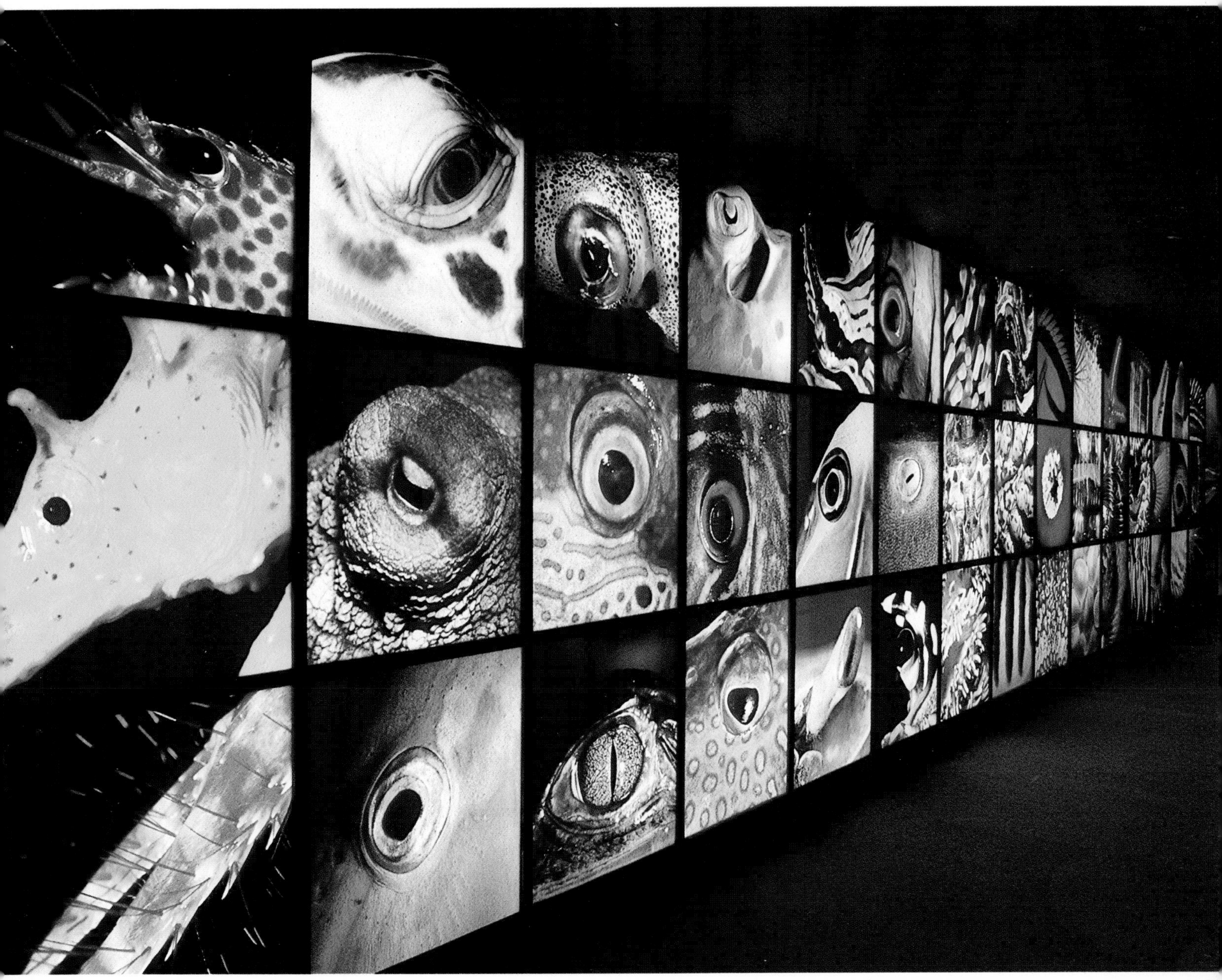

exhibitor: Urban Council of Hong Kong
designer: Landor Associates
producer: General Exhibits, Inc.

The Hong Kong Space Museum is currently the world's most complete museum of astronomy and space with more than 50 major exhibits and five theaters.